Acknowledgements and Copyright Laws

Lizard Learning Pty Ltd
GPO Box 1941, Brisbane, Queensland, 4001
ABN: 13 158 235 333
www.lizardlearning.com

Copyright © Lizard Learning 2017
Edition 1

Publisher: Lizard Learning Pty Ltd
Content Writers: Cindy Holmberg-Smith, Rema Whyte, Carmen Kleindeinst, Cassandra Potts, Elizabeth Beames, Rebekka Curnow
Content Editors: Cindy Holmberg-Smith, Barbara Stewart, Sue Okely, Danielle Freeman, Carmen Kleindeinst
Digital Formatter: New Wave Design
Cover Design: Book Cover Cafe, New Wave Design
Illustrators: Trevor Salter, Book Cover Cafe, Aleisha Coffey, New Wave Design
Project Managers: Cindy Holmberg-Smith, Anthony Puttee
Administration Officers / Desktop Operators: Natalie Pugsley, Dylan Holmberg

Reproduction and communication for other purposes
Except as permitted under the Act (for example a fair dealing for the purposes of study, research, criticism, or review), no part of this book may be reproduced, stored in a retrieval system, communicated or transmitted in any form or by any means without prior written permission. All enquiries should be made to the publisher at the address above.

Blackline Master - This master may only be reproduced by the original purchaser for use with their class. The publisher prohibits the loaning or onselling of the master for purposes of reproduction.

All rights reserved.

ISBN: 978-1-925509-61-8

Contents

Year 1	8 – 17
Year 2	20 – 29
Year 3	32 – 41
Year 4	44 – 53
Year 5	56 – 65
Year 6	68 – 77
Answers	78 – 83

Year 1

Activity Pages: 8 – 17
Answers: 78

| Name: | Date: | Year: |

1. Rewrite this sentence with the correct **punctuation** and **spelling**:

   my grandma lives in melbourne _____

   _____

2. **Can you remember the meaning of adjectives to complete this question?**
   Adjectives are describin _____ words.

3. **Word endings are a letter or group of letters placed at the end of a word:**
   (e.g. jump - jumping, block - blocks). Write **-s** on the end of **head**: _____

4. **Rearrange** these words to make a proper sentence: my The stung bee friend. buzzing

   _____

5. **Writing Time!** Finish this sentence: The plane... _____

   _____

   a) at the airport took off.   b) stomped through the desert.

6. What time does the teacher's clock show right now? _____
   What was the time **8 hours** ago? _____

7. Write the **missing numbers**, think of the hundreds board:

   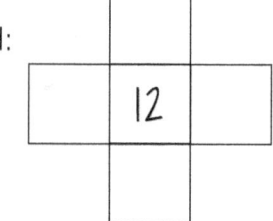

8. Write the missing number in the **addition sentence**: 2 + _____ = 12

9. Which object is **heavier**? _____

   A   B

10. 15 kittens in a box and two were taken out. How many left in the box?_____

10 Quick Questions a Day | www.lizardlearning.com

| Name: | Date: | Year: |

1. Rewrite this sentence with the correct **punctuation** and **spelling**:

   he waz a farma who grew lettuce carrots end peas

   _____

   _____

2. Write the word that is spelled **correctly**:

   I didn't know _____ (**witch** / **which**) way to turn, left or right.

3. *Plurals are words that mean more than one.*

   Draw something that you can make more than one or **plural**. Have a go at spelling this word and check with an adult.

   e.g.  You would draw 2 or more apples.

4. *Synonyms are words that have similar meanings.* Write a word from the box that is similar to **meal**: | neat   dinner   harm   weep | _____

5. *Writing time!* My favourite game is... _____

6. What time does the teacher's clock show right now? _____

   What will be the time **9 hours** from now? _____

7. Write the number of butterflies beside each jar, then write if it is an **even** or **odd** number:

   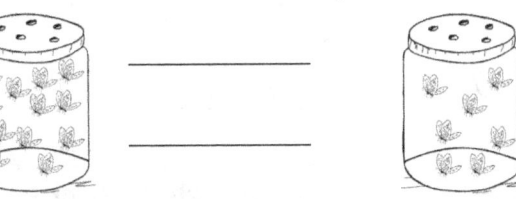

8. Which house shape won the **most** points? _____

   Athletic's Day
   Number of points won for each house

9. Using your eraser, measure the **length** of your homework book: _____

10. 18 dragons plus 2 more. How many now? _____

Name: _____ Date: _____ Year: _____

1. Rewrite this sentence with the correct **punctuation** and **spelling**:

    the vase was olde and haid a crack, a chip, a scrach and a marke on it

    _____

    _____

2. ***A pronoun is a word that takes the place of a noun (e.g. her, him, it, themselves).***

    Write one **pronoun**: _____

3. Write **do**, **does** or **did** on the line to make the sentence correct:

    _____ you see the koala in the tree at the park yesterday?

4. ***Antonyms are words that are opposites.***

    Use a word from the box to write the **antonym** for **day**: | morning   new   night   rich |

    _____

5. Write words from the box that begin with the letter **a**: _____

    | animal   empty   kite   an   cat   jog   naughty   kitten   and   nice   a   church |

6. What time does the teacher's clock show right now? _____

    What was the time **9 hours** ago? _____

7. My sister is turning 8 today, draw more candles on the cake to make **8**.

    How many more candles did you draw? _____

8. Write the next **two** numbers: 29 _____ _____ 32

9. Practise singing this rhyme. Can you write the **missing number** in the box below?

    Calendar Rhyme
    [   ] days have September, April, June and November. All the rest have 31 except for February alone, which has 28 days clear but 29 days in each leap year.

10. *Challenge!* 27 apples in a bowl and two were eaten.

    How many apples were left? _____

10 Quick Questions a Day | www.lizardlearning.com

| Name: | Date: | Year: |

1. Rewrite this sentence with the correct **punctuation** and **spelling**:

    the lampp was pritty with a hooge yelowe shade

    _____

    _____

2. **Nouns are the names of people, places, animals or things.**

    Which **noun** does this picture show?   monster   bread   vest   _____

3. **Contractions are shortened forms of two words.**

    Write the correct **short way** for: could not _____

4. **Homophones are two or more words that sound the same but have different meanings and spelling (e.g. right/write).** Write the correct **homophone** in this sentence:

    Dad had to _____ (break / brake) really hard before we hit the gutter.

5. Write one animal that starts with the letter **m**: _____

6. What time does the teacher's clock show right now? _____

    What will be the time **10 hours** from now? _____

7. 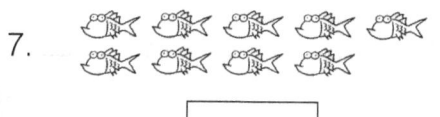 and 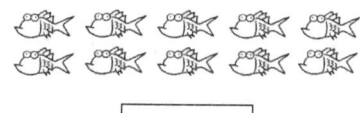 makes 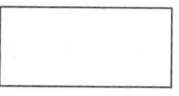 fish

    [ ]   +   [ ]   =   [ ]

8. Who is sitting in the **front left row**? _____

    FRONT

    | Billy | Tia |
    | Jed | Emma |
    | Oliver | Jasper |
    | Kate | Tina |

    LEFT / RIGHT

    BACK

9. How many children in the classroom today? _____

    Would this amount of children fit on your kitchen table? _____

10. 17 cups plus 2 more. How many now? _____

Name: _____ Date: _____ Year: _____

1. Rewrite this sentence with the correct **punctuation** and **spelling**:
   can you quickly come hear penny
   _____

2. **Verbs are doing / action words.** Write the **verb** in this sentence:
   I cut the paper in half. _____

3. Which pair of words **rhyme**?   sea / flea   boy / plate
   Write the **rhyming pair** when you find them: _____

4. **There are three articles: the, a and an. The, is a definite article (e.g. give me the cup). A, is an indefinite article (e.g. give me a cup. This would be any cup). An, is the article to use before a vowel (e.g. an umbrella).**
   In the box below, match **a**, **an** or **the** with these words: ride / trolley / ape

a	an	the

5. Make a **list** of things you might need from the **supermarket**: _____
   _____

6. What time does the teacher's clock show right now? _____
   What was the time **10 hours** ago? _____

7. Sheldon the shark eats 2 of everything. Cross out what he eats. Write how many are left altogether
    _____

8. Write the **chance** that you will have cabbage for dinner tonight:
   a) will happen   b) won't happen   c) might happen _____

9. **Draw** 1 hexagon and 2 ovals:

10. 17 oranges on the tree and 4 were picked. How many are left? _____

10 Quick Questions a Day | www.lizardlearning.com

Name:	Date:	Year:

1. Rewrite this sentence with the correct **punctuation** and **spelling**:

   he opend the frunt door and the dog jumpped up on him _____

   _____

2. **Adjectives are describing words.** Write an **adjective** in this sentence:

   The _____ elephant stomped on my teacher's foot.

3. **Word endings are a letter or group of letters placed at the end of a word:**

   (e.g. jump - jumping, block - blocks). Write **-ing** on the end of **skip**: _____

4. Write the nearest meaning to the word **head**: _____

         a) the top of your body   **b)** a smelly food

5. Write one animal that starts with the letter **o**: _____

6. What time does the teacher's clock show right now? _____

   What will be the time **1 hour** from now? _____

7. How many 1 dollar coins can you count? _____

   How much money is there altogether? _____

8. Write the missing numbers in the **addition sentence**: _____ + _____ = 15

🦀 🦀 🦀 🦀 🦀 🦀 🦀 🦀 🦀	🦀 🦀 🦀 🦀 🦀 🦀

9. In which **month** does Mrs Fran retire? _____

School Events Calendar					
January	February	March	April	May	June
26th Australia Day			10th Easter Bonnet Parade 2.00pm		
July	August	September	October	November	December
	31st Mrs Fran's Retirement Parade			11th Remembrance Day Parade	13th Christmas Carols Parade 14th Break up Day

10. 15 ties plus 2 more. How many now? _____

| Name: | Date: | Year: |

1. Rewrite this sentence with the correct **punctuation** and **spelling**:

   the babies of a kangaroo and a koala are called joeys.

   _____

   _____

2. ***Nouns are the names of people, places, animals or things.***

   Write the **place** from the **list**: _____

    bedroom    dog   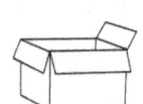 box

3. ***Contractions are shortened forms of two words.***

   Write one **contraction**: _____

4. ***Antonyms are words that are opposites.*** Use a word from the box to write the **opposite** of

   quiet: _____ | found   happy   noisy   right |

5. 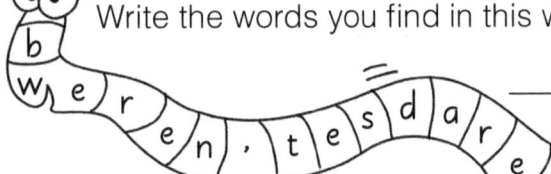 Write the words you find in this word worm: _____

   _____

   _____

6. What time does the teacher's clock show right now? _____

   What was the time **2 hours** ago? _____

7. **Join** the pig to the answers:

8. Write the position of the **cylinder**: _____

9. How many children in the classroom today? _____

   Would this amount of children fit in your bedroom? _____

10. 73 boats were in the water. Count back 1. How many boats left? _____

Name: _____ Date: _____ Year: _____

1. Rewrite this sentence with the correct **punctuation**:

   paula couldnt stop laughing it was such a funny movie

   _____

   _____

2. **Adjectives are describing words.**

   Write the missing **adjective** then draw a picture to show

   a _____ flower.

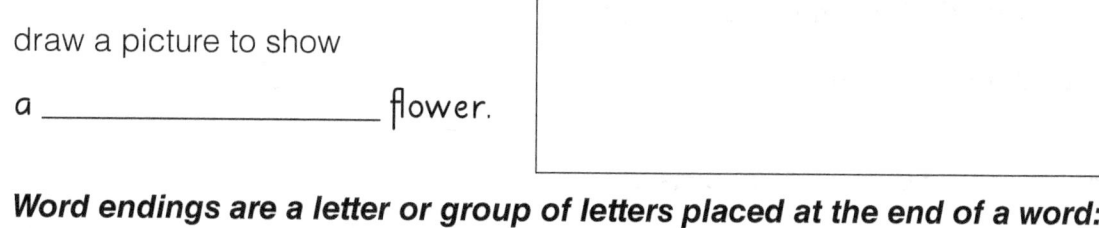

3. **Word endings are a letter or group of letters placed at the end of a word:** **(e.g. jump - jumping, block - blocks).** Write **-s** on the end of these words:

   bowl ___   run ___   tree ___

4. **Synonyms are words that have similar meanings.**

   | rabbit   huge   pond   speak |

   Write a word from the box that is **similar** to **talk**: _____

5. **Vowels are A E I O U. Consonants are all the other letters of the alphabet.**

   Write the missing **consonants** in this word: *Clue: it's a number*   ___ ___ ___ e e

6. What time does the teacher's clock show right now? _____

   What will be the time **11 hours** from now? _____

7. Write the **value** of this coin:  _____

8. Write the missing number in the **addition sentence**: _____ + _____ = 18

   | 🦎🦎🦎🦎🦎🦎🦎🦎🦎🦎 | 🦎🦎 |

9. Using your sharpener, measure the **length** of your book: _____

10. 88 cherries were in the box and 7 were eaten. How many cherries left? _____

Name: _____   **Date:** _____   **Year:** _____

1. Rewrite this sentence with the correct **punctuation** and **spelling**:

   watch out four the cars

   _____

2. Write the word that is spelled **correctly**:

   Nathan's _____ (coff / cough) seemed to be getting better everyday.

3. ***Plurals are words that mean more than one.***

   Add **-s** or **-es** to **house** to make it **plural**: _____

4. ***Antonyms are words that are opposites.***

   Using a word from the box write the an **antonym** for **wide**: _____

   | first | found | narrow | happy | hard | noisy | rough | right |

5. ***Writing Time!*** Finish this sentence: The noise was so loud it... _____

   _____

6. What time does the teacher's clock show right now? _____

   What was the time **11 hours** ago? _____

7. Write the **missing numbers**:

   Clue: think of the hundreds board.

7	8		10
	19		

8. How many **shapes** are there altogether?

   _____

   Spell the number: _____

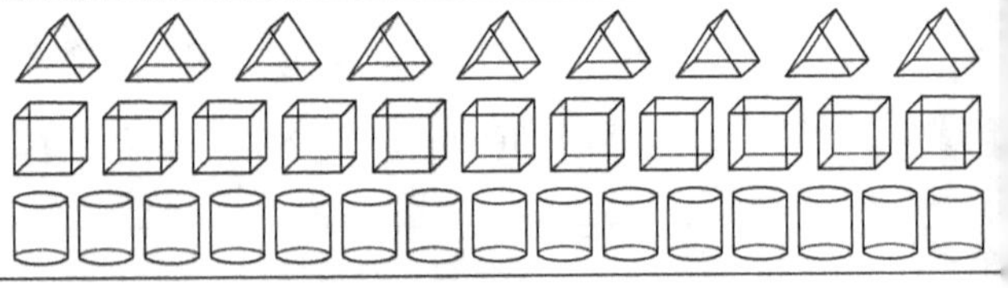

   Bryce △△△△△△△△
   Nora ◻◻◻◻◻◻◻◻◻◻
   Evan ⌭⌭⌭⌭⌭⌭⌭⌭⌭⌭⌭

9. Which object has a **larger mass**? _____   A   B

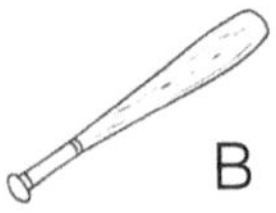

10. 50 crabs plus 9. How many now? _____

Name: _____ Date: _____ Year: _____

1. Rewrite this sentence with the correct **punctuation** and **spelling**:
   they're hous had thre bedrooms
   _____

2. **Verbs are doing / action words.** What **verb** does this picture show?
   skid   squeeze   pull   _____

3. Write words from the box that **rhyme** with **matter**: _____
   _____

   batter   your   have   chatter   large   patter   scatter

4. Write the nearest meaning to **quick**: _____
   a) to move fast   **b)** hot to touch

5. Write the capital letter for: v ____   e ____   f ____   g ____   j ____

6. What time does the teacher's clock show right now? _____
   What will be the time **1 hour** from now? _____

7.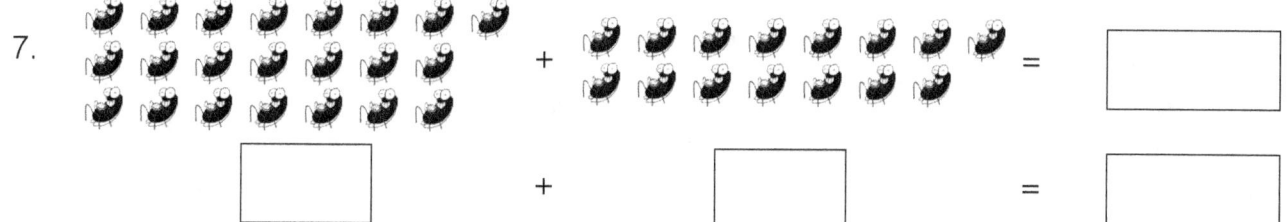

8. **Draw** something that **won't** happen tonight:

   [ ]

9. How many children in the classroom today? _____
   Would this amount of children fit into your backyard? _____

10. 26 flowers plus 3 more. How many now? _____

Year 2

Activity Pages: 20 – 29
Answers: 78 – 79

Name: _____ Date: _____ Year: _____

1. Rewrite this sentence with the correct **punctuation** and **spelling**:
   chickens are birds but dont fly muche and emus cant fly at all
   _____
   _____

2. *An adverb is a word which modifies or adds meaning to a verb, adjective or adverb by telling how, when, why or where a thing is done.* Write the **adverb** in this sentence:
   The duckling was quickly following its mum across the busy road. _____

3. *A suffix is a letter or group of letters placed after or at the end of a word to change its meaning.* Write **-ing** on the end of **drop** (*remember the rule*): _____

4. *Homophones are two or more words that sound the same but have different meanings and spelling (e.g. right/write).* Write the **homophone** for **hair**: hare / where _____

5. *(Say the word).* Write on the line how many **syllables/sounds** you hear, then put these words into **alphabetical** order: _____

train	baby	bulldozer
_____	_____	_____

   a b c d e f g h i j k l m n o p q r s t u v w x y z

6. What time does the teacher's clock show right now? _____
   What will be the time **2 hours 45 minutes** from now? _____

7. Use your calculator to write the symbols used: 38 ☐ 14 ☐ 52
   38 birds on the wire and 14 more joined them. How many birds in total? _____

8.
   ```
     697
   + 102
   ─────
   ```

   Calendar Rhyme
   30 days have September April, June and November. All the rest have 31 except for February alone, which has 28 days clear but 29 days in each leap year.

9. Say the calendar rhyme **5** times.

10. There are 21 milk bottles on 3 steps. How many milk bottles to a step? _____

Name: _____ Date: _____ Year: _____

1. Rewrite this sentence with the correct **punctuation** and **spelling**:

   hey you _____

2. **Can you remember what a preposition is?** Write the **preposition** you see:

   Down the road ran the naughty boy. _____

3. **A prefix is a letter or group of letters placed before or in front of a word to change its meaning (e.g. un, re, mis).** Write the word that has the **prefix** that matches the meaning:

   To take a cover off: recover / uncover / uncoverable   _____

4. **Rearrange** these words to make a proper sentence: the to write a white paper note.

   Mason used _____

5. Make a **list** of things you might need to **go fishing**: _____
   _____

6. What time does the teacher's clock show right now? _____

   Challenge! Lucy read her book **2 hours** on Monday, **3 and a half hours** on Wednesday and **three quarters of an hour** on Friday. How many hours did Lucy read for? _____

7. Write the **odd** numbers that you see in this picture:

60	62	90	48
2	13	69	86	97

   _____

8. How many birthdays altogether in **January**, **July** and **December**? _____

   Which is your favourite month? _____ Why? _____

Class Birthdays					
January	February	March	April	May	June
🧁🧁🧁🧁🧁	🧁	🧁🧁🧁🧁	🧁🧁🧁🧁🧁	🧁🧁🧁	🧁
July	August	September	October	November	December
🧁🧁	🧁🧁🧁🧁	🧁🧁🧁🧁🧁🧁	🧁🧁	🧁🧁🧁🧁	🧁🧁🧁🧁🧁

9. **Draw** what this shape would look like **flipped**:

10. How much money is shown in the picture? 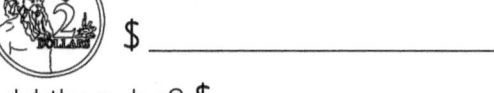 $ _____

    If 50 cents was spent, how much change would there be? $ _____

Name: _____ Date: _____ Year: _____

1. Rewrite this sentence with the correct **punctuation** and **spelling**:

   in june im going to get a new bike replied charlie _____
   _____

2. **Nouns are the names of people, places, animals or things.** Draw a **noun** you would find at the **circus**:

3. Write **has** or **have** into the sentence to make it correct.

   You _____ strawberry jam on your shirt.

4. *There are three articles: the, a and an. The, is a definite article (e.g. give me the cup). A, is an indefinite article (e.g. give me a cup. This would be any cup). An, is the article to use before a vowel (e.g. an umbrella).*

   Write these words in the box below with the correct **article**: plane / elephant / shop

a	an	the
_____	_____	_____

5. Write the letter that comes after J: _____

6. What time does the teacher's clock show right now? _____
   What will be the time **3 hours 15 minutes** from now? _____

7. 2 groups of 4 papers = _____
   _____ × _____ = _____

   Make your own to match:

8. Make your own **number pattern**: _____ _____ _____ _____ _____

9. **Draw** a picture of something in the classroom which has **parallel lines**:

10. How many groups of three monsters are there in this picture? _____

10 Quick Questions a Day | www.lizardlearning.com

1. Rewrite this sentence with the correct **punctuation** and **spelling**:

   the childrun saw the bear scratching his back on the tre by the rivur

   _____

   _____

2. **Verbs are doing / action words.** Write one **verb** you would do in your **bed**: _____

3. Read this sentence. Write if it is **past**, **present** or **future** tense: Emma will be going to grandma's beach house. _____

4. What is the nearest meaning to the word **letter**: _____

   _____

   a) to send a message to someone   b) in the backyard to keep you cool in summer

5. Write the words you find in this word worm: _____

   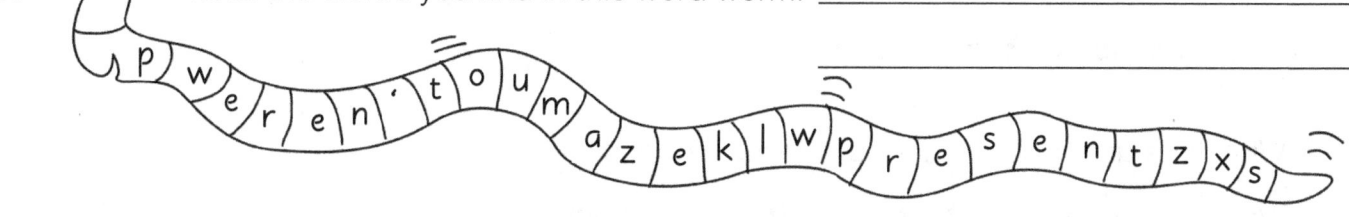

   _____

6. What time does the teacher's clock show right now? _____

   How many minutes between **two thirty** in the afternoon and **3:30pm**? _____

7. 10 + 3 = _____   13 - 3 = _____   13 - 10 = _____   3 + 10 = _____

8. Starting at the **parallel lines**, move left 2 places and up 1 place.

   What is this shape? _____

   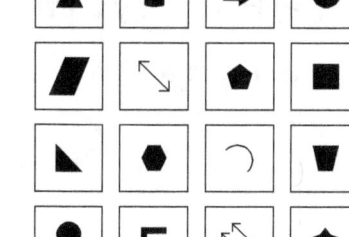

9. **Match** the shape with the word:

   Hexagon   Oval   Circle

10. If Lily brushes her teeth once every day, how many times will she brush her teeth in December? _____

Name: _____ Date: _____ Year: _____

1. Rewrite this sentence with the correct **punctuation** and **spelling**:

   birds can be many colours such as green blue red and even rainbow coloured

   _____

   _____

2. ***Adjectives are describing words.*** Write the **adjective** in this sentence:

   When I looked up to the _____ sky, it was raining.

3. ***Compound words are two or more words joined together to form a new word (e.g. seashell).*** Join these two smaller words to make a **compound** word:

   light + house = _____

4. What are you going to be when you **grow up**? _____

5. ***Vowels are A E I O U. Consonants are all the other letters of the alphabet.*** Write the missing **consonants** in this day of the week: ___ e ___ ___ e ___ ___ a ___

6. What time does the teacher's clock show right now? _____

   What will be the time **3 hours 45 minutes** from now? _____

7. Spell this ordinal number **5th**: _____

8. What is the **chance** that your PE teacher will be sitting in a tree today? _____

9. **a)** How many **corners** does this shape have? _____

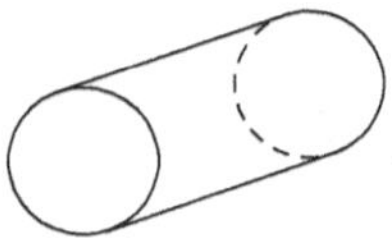

   b) Draw a picture of a shape with 6 **faces**:

10. 20 erasers were given to the class. 1 eraser had to be shared between 2 students. How many students were there in the class? _____

Name: _____ Date: _____ Year: _____

1. Rewrite this sentence with the correct **punctuation** and **spelling**:
   the dog just bit me yelled joseph
   _____
   _____

2. Write the mouse sound that is spelled **correctly**: "Squeak, sqweek" the mouse said.
   _____

3. **Contractions are shortened forms of two words.**
   Write the correct **contraction** for: is not _____

4. **Synonyms are words that have similar meanings.** Think of a word and write a word that is **similar**. Write each word: _____

5. **Writing time!** Finish this sentence: Henry was crying as… _____
   _____

6. What time does the teacher's clock show right now? _____
   What will be the time in **15 minutes** from now? _____

7. Write the **even** numbers you see in the pig's belly:

8. 13 = _____ + _____   19 = _____ + _____

9. Complete the **missing month**:

   Calendar Rhyme
   30 days have September, April, June and _____ . All the rest have 31 except for February alone, which has 28 days clear but 29 days in each leap year.

10. Mary had 86 lollies. She gave away 27 lollies to her friends. How many lollies did Mary have left? _____

Name: _____ Date: _____ Year: _____

1. Rewrite this sentence with the correct **punctuation**:

   im not well harry said to his teacher mrs roberts _____

   _____

2. **A pronoun is a word that takes the place of a noun (e.g. her, him, it, themselves).**

   Write a sentence with one **pronoun** included: _____

   _____

3. Write a word from the box that **rhymes** with **bird**: _____

   navy   ground   clover   heard   hand   rag   moon

4. **Can you remember the meaning of antonyms to complete this question?** Think of a word and write a word that is **opposite**. Write each word: _____

5. Put a line through or write the word for the picture that **doesn't belong**: _____

    mobile    laptop    ice cream    computer mouse

6. What time does the teacher's clock show right now? _____

   What will be the time **45 minutes** from now? _____

7.
   ```
     976          35
   +   8        - 10
   _____        _____

     419          476
   +  43        -   8
   _____        _____
   ```

2 F's Lunchbox Survey					
	Apple	Sandwich	Salad Wrap	Muffin	Tuckshop
Monday	8				
Tuesday		14			
Wednesday				7	
Thursday				15	
Friday					18

8. On which day was the **least** popular food found in lunch boxes? _____

   What is the **difference** in muffins to apples? _____

9. Have these fish been **flipped**, **slid** or **turned**? _____

10. How many groups of 3 in 18? _____

Name: Date: Year:

1. Rewrite this sentence with the correct **punctuation** and **spelling**:

    the beach was very very dark at niht but thay werent scarred

    _____

    _____

2. *An adverb is a word which modifies or adds meaning to a verb, adjective or adverb by telling how, when, why or where a thing is done.* Write four **adverbs**: _____

    _____

3. *A suffix is a letter or group of letters placed after or at the end of a word to change its meaning.* Write -ed on the end of **dress** and write this new word in a sentence: _____

    _____

4. *Can you remember the meaning of homophones to complete this question?*
    Write the **homophone** for **heal**:   heel / need   _____

5. Write the word that has the same sound as **q**: quick / old / purple _____

6. What time does the teacher's clock show right now? _____
    Ava the newborn baby, slept for **four hours** at her 1st nap, **three hours** at her 2nd nap and **five hours** at her afternoon nap. How many hours altogether did she sleep that day?

    _____

7. 17 + 7 = _____   34 - 17 = _____   34 - 7 = _____   7 + 17 = _____

8. Write the number **before** and **after** the number in the circle: ( )   799   ( )

9. Which picture has **parallel lines**?

    _____

    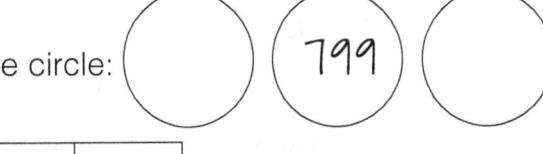

                     sheep   soccer field

10. Jason invited 10 friends to his Starwars party. All of his friends who were invited came along with a friend of their own. How many people were at the party? _____

| Name: | Date: | Year: |

1. Rewrite this sentence with the correct **punctuation** and **spelling**:
   kangaroos wallibies koalas and wombats are not domestik animals tht live in our bakyards as peets _____
   _____

2. *Can you remember the meaning of prepositions to complete this question?*
   Write the **preposition** you see: over the hill _____

3. *A prefix is a letter or group of letters placed before or in front of a word to change its meaning (e.g. un, re, mis).* Correctly add the **prefix im**, **un** or **re** to possible: _____

4. **Rearrange** these words to make a proper sentence: it hot. like I water drink to when is
   _____

5. Make a **list** of things you would need to play a game of **cricket**: _____
   _____

6. What time does the teacher's clock show right now? _____
   Keith was on holidays. He went fishing for **six and a half hours** on Saturday and **nine and a half hours** on Sunday. How long did Keith fish altogether? _____

7. What order is the **bird** coming?
   _____

8. What number would the monkey land on if he jumped backward **three** spaces? _____

   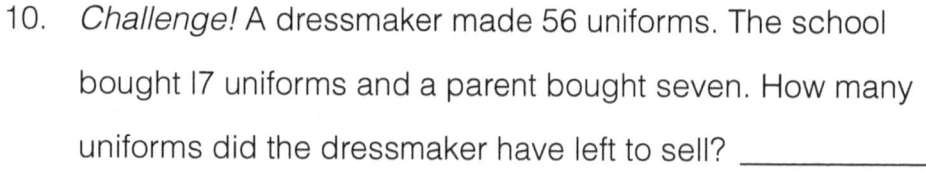
   618   61   378   916   222   483   950   1000   799

9. Write your **initials** in the circles, colour the rectangles **red** and the triangles **blue**:

10. *Challenge!* A dressmaker made 56 uniforms. The school bought 17 uniforms and a parent bought seven. How many uniforms did the dressmaker have left to sell? _____

10 Quick Questions a Day | www.lizardlearning.com

1. Rewrite this sentence with the correct **punctuation**:

   stop shouting _____

2. **Can you remember the meaning of nouns to complete this task?**

   Draw a **noun** found at the **zoo**:

   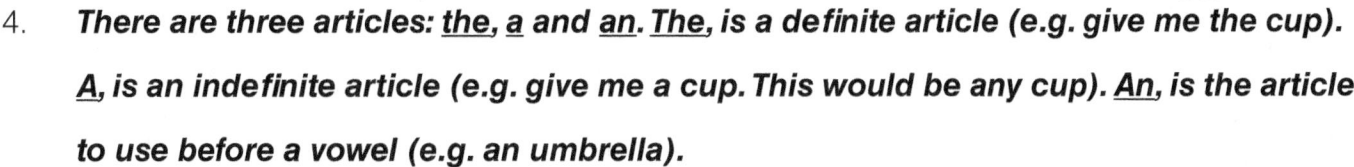

3. Write **these** or **those** into the sentence to make it correct:

   There are _____ pictures we were looking for.

4. **There are three articles: <u>the</u>, <u>a</u> and <u>an</u>. <u>The</u>, is a definite article (e.g. give me the cup). <u>A</u>, is an indefinite article (e.g. give me a cup. This would be any cup). <u>An</u>, is the article to use before a vowel (e.g. an umbrella).**

   Write the word that fits (**a**, **an** or **the**): _____ lemon and orange are both hard to eat.

5. Write the **capital** letters for these: h _____   l _____   r _____   v _____

6. What time does the teacher's clock show right now? _____

   What will be the time **1 hour 15 minutes** from now? _____

7. Draw **MAB blocks** to match the number: 945

8. **Draw** something that **won't** happen on the weekend:

9. Write two **2D** shapes that you see in this picture: _____

10. Ben received 2 grapes from his friend Cooper. Ava gave Ben ten times as many grapes as Cooper gave him. How many grapes did Ava give Ben? _____

Year 3

Activity Pages: 32 – 41
Answers: 79 – 80

Name: _____ Date: _____ Year: _____

1. Rewrite this sentence with the correct **punctuation** and **spelling**:

   once apon a time a fairy lived in a majic land far far away _____
   _____

2. **Can you remember the meaning of proper nouns to complete this question?**

   Write the definition of proper **nouns**: _____
   _____

3. **A suffix is a letter or group of letters placed after or at the end of a word to change its meaning.** Add the **suffix -ing**, **-er** and **–ed** to the word **crack**: _____

4. **A homograph is a word that has the same spelling but a different meaning (e.g. fine/fine) and sometimes a different sound (e.g. tear/tear).** Write two meanings for the **homograph** word:

   dribble: _____
   dribble: _____

5. What smaller word can be found in the word **beach**? _____

6. What time does the teacher's clock show right now? _____

   What will be the time **30 minutes** from now? _____

7. Colour $\frac{7}{8}$ of the boxes: ☐☐☐☐☐☐☐☐

8. Five people went to a pie factory. The results of what was eaten, and by whom, is as follows:

Pie Eating Contest				
Person	Apple Pie	Peach Pie	Apricot Pie	Rhubarb Pie
Sandra	3	2	5	4
Karla	1	3	2	1
Andrew	5	3	2	0
Colin	6	2	1	1
Nicole	3	1	3	2

   How **many** pies did Karla eat? _____ Did Colin eat **more** than Sandra? _____

9. How many more cubes need to be added to give a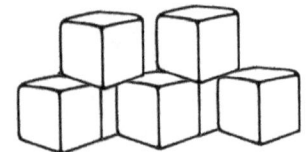

   volume of 12 cubes? _____

10. 68 bricks were needed to go on 2 walls. How many bricks needed for each wall? _____

10 Quick Questions a Day | www.lizardlearning.com

Name: _____ Date: _____ Year: _____

1. Rewrite this sentence with the correct **punctuation** and **spelling**:
   the smalst bone in the humin bodie kan be fnd in tha eer
   _____

2. *Can you remember the meaning of nouns to complete this question?*
   A noun is the name of people, _____, _____ or _____ .

3. *Compound words are two or more words joined together to form a new word (e.g. seashell).* Write a **compound** word: _____

4. *Homophones are two or more words that sound the same but have different meanings and spelling (e.g. right/write).* Write the **homophones** for:
   board _____ bawl _____

5. *Vowels are A E I O U. Consonants are all the other letters of the alphabet.*
   Fill in the missing **vowels** in the following word: t ___ ___ c h ___ r

6. What time does the teacher's clock show right now? _____
   The time is **7:25am**. Write the time in **three and a half** hours: _____
   Write this new time on the clock face:

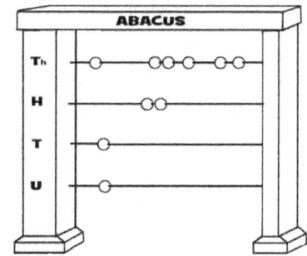

7. Write the number displayed on the **abacus**: _____

8. Complete the pattern: 950 850 _____ _____ _____

9. *Area measures the size of a surface. Square centimetres is the measure used for small surfaces (e.g. the desk top). Square metres is used for larger surfaces (e.g. a football field). Formula for Area = Length x Width. 1cm² = 1cm x 1cm. A = L x W.*
   Write the shape that has an area **greater** than B:

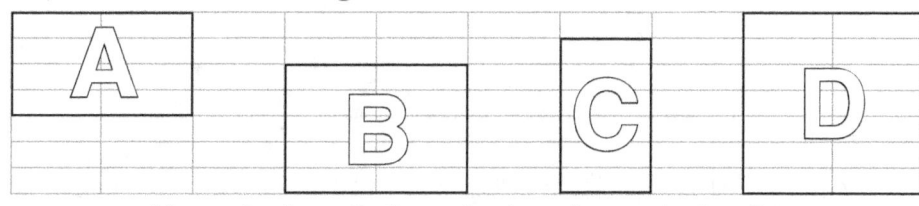

10. How many groups of four ducks are there in the picture below? _____

10 Quick Questions a Day | www.lizardlearning.com

| Name: | Date: | Year: |

1. Rewrite this sentence with the correct **punctuation** and **spelling**:
   pearl waved goodby to her pairents _____
   _____

2. **Can you remember the meaning of pronouns to complete this question?**
   Pronouns take _____

3. **Plurals are words that mean more than one.** Write the **plurals** for:
   woman _____ teacher _____ uncle _____

4. Insert the **correct** word: Is that _____ (your / you're) magazine?

5. Write four weekly spelling words in **alphabetical** order: _____
   _____

6. What time does the teacher's clock show right now? _____
   What will be the time **40 minutes** from now? _____

7. Write the **even** numbers: _____
   1327, 41, 3219, 273, 3609, 1111, 42, 888, 316, 639, 502, 4722

8. Emma rolled a die 13 times. These are her results:
   6 5 2 6 3 1 2 4 5 3 6 4 2
   Complete the table below using the data collected from Emma's die. The first one has been done for you:

Outcome of die roll	Number Of Times Rolled		
	Once	Twice	Three Times
One	✓		
Two			
Three			
Four			
Five			

9. How many **cm** in a **m**? _____

10. The Ashgrove Soccer Club's Under 8's team scored 38 points at the end of the season. They needed 69 points to be the overall champions. Did they become the champions? If not, by how many points did they miss out? _____

Name: _____ Date: _____ Year: _____

1. Rewrite this sentence with the correct **punctuation** and **spelling**:
   marilyn had three litle broters called mike ben and billy
   _____
   _____

2. *A pronoun is a word that takes the place of a noun (e.g. her, him, its, themselves).*
   Write the correct **pronoun** in the sentence:
   Mary said _____ (**she** / **them**) doesn't like potatoes.

3. *Contractions are shortened forms of two words.* Write the long version of the **contraction** in this sentence: <u>Let's</u> go and play a fun game together. _____

4. *Antonyms are words that are opposites.* Write the **antonym** to **found**: ____ o ____ ____

5. Write the **adjective/s** that match the picture:
   _____
   _____

dangerous
curious   carnivore
fluffier   whiskers
rainforest

6. What time does the teacher's clock show right now? _____
   Write this time on the clock face: **8:40**

7. 762 - 48 = _____

8. Draw the **next** picture in the pattern:

  _____ _____ _____

9. This jug holds **1 litre** of water.
   Draw this jug and show what
   half a litre of water would look like:

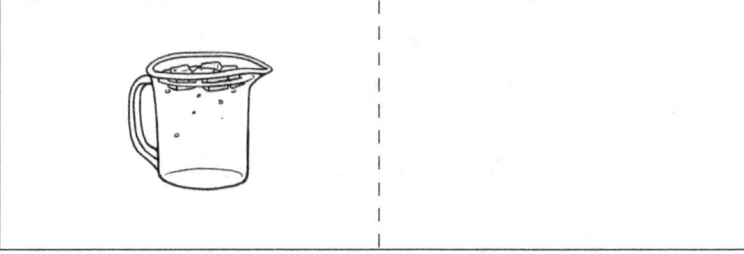

10. Thursday's temperature was 34 degrees. Friday will be 5 degrees lower. What will the temperature be on Friday? _____

Name: _____ Date: _____ Year: _____

1. Rewrite this sentence with the correct **punctuation** and **spelling**:

    phillipa luved the storys that her granmuther wuld tel her at bedtim each nite

    _____

    _____

    _____

2. ***Plurals are words that mean more than one.*** Write the **plurals** for:

    story _____   try _____   lady _____

3. ***Can you remember the meaning of pronouns to complete this question?***

    Write the definition of **pronouns**: _____

    _____

4. Write the **correct** word into the sentence:

    I was _____ (**to / too / two**) excited to sleep before the excursion.

5. **Rearrange** these words in **alphabetical** order: travel / table / adventure / ordinary

    _____

6. What time does the teacher's clock show right now? _____

    What will be the time **50 minutes** from now? _____

7. **True** or **False**? 70 ÷ 10 = 7 groups of 10 _____

8. Complete the pattern: 400 500 _____ _____ _____ _____ _____

9. Which stick would fit inside the **base C**? _____

    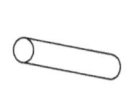

    stick A   stick B   stick C   base A   base B   base C

10. The take away shop had 263 boxes of biscuits to sell in the months of January, February and March. They sold 120 boxes. How many more boxes of biscuits did they have to sell?

    _____

Name: _____ Date: _____ Year: _____

1. Rewrite this sentence with the correct **punctuation** and **spelling**:
   mum gav me an gingerbred man a glass of milk and an bannana fore afternoon tea _____
   _____

2. *Can you remember the meaning of adverb to complete this question?*
   Write the definition of **adverbs**: _____

3. *A prefix is a letter or group of letters placed before or in front of a word to change its meaning (e.g. un, re, mis).* Rewrite **tangle**, **paid** and **side** using the **prefixes** from the box:
   | pre in un | _____

4. *Homophones are two or more words that sound the same but have different meanings and spelling (e.g. right/write).* Write **homophones** for:
   raise: _____   hire: _____
   Write all **homophones** in sentences: _____
   _____
   _____

5. Write the **odd** word out: | cook hot food boat stove | _____

6. What time does the teacher's clock show right now? _____
   What will be the time **9 hours and 10 minutes** from now? _____

7. *Challenge!*
   ```
     600          300         1376         8604
   -  95        -  42       +  948       + 1798
   _____        _____       _____       _____
   ```

8. Write the **chance** your principal will wear a Santa Clause outfit this Christmas:
   impossible, likely, possible or certain _____

9. Which of these objects would **measure** capacity? _____
    jug    dog    envelope    table

10. There are 55 goldfish in 11 tanks. How many goldfish are there in each tank? _____

| Name: | Date: | Year: |

1. Rewrite this sentence with the correct **punctuation** and **spelling**:
   kate went too the lack and sore three frogs two lizards five birds and six fish
   _____
   _____

2. *Can you remember the meaning of pronouns to complete this question?*
   Write the correct **pronoun** in this sentence:
   Did_____ (you / them) remember to feed the dog?

3. Rewrite this sentence using the **correct** spelling:
   The little worm had to rigle its way out from the deliteful orange. _____
   _____

4. *Antonyms are words that are opposites.* Write the **antonym** for **pretty**: _____

5. *Writing Time!* Finish this sentence: My friend and I were trapped in a... _____
   _____

6. What time does the teacher's clock show right now? _____
   Write **12:25** on the clock face:

7. Write the number: 40 000 + 2000 + 500 + 60 + 1 = _____

8. Which image is **closest** to the hotdog? _____
   Which **direction** is correct moving from the chocolate
   to the burger?   **a)** Right 1, Up 3   **b)** Up 4, Right Three
   _____

9. Do you remember the calendar rhyme?
   Test someone near you to see if they know it.

10. A box contained 66 kilograms of washing powder. After 49 kilograms had been used what
    amount remained? _____

| Name: | Date: | Year: |

1. Rewrite this sentence with the correct **punctuation** and **spelling**:
   dont forget your hat ball and spade called sandras dad _____
   _____

2. ***Verbs are doing / action words.*** Write the **verb** in this sentence:
   Peter was sweeping the floor. _____

3. ***Compound words are two or more words joined together to form a new word (e.g. seashell).*** Using **boat / saw / to** complete the **compound** words:
   sail_____ in_____ see _____

4. ***Can you remember the meaning of homophones to complete this question?***
   Write the correct **homophone** into the sentence:
   I will have _____ (to / too / two) please.
   Write a sentence using the other two **homophones**: _____
   _____

5. Rewrite **dry** in the **past**, **present** and **future tense**: Yesterday I _____
   Today I _____ Tomorrow I shall _____

6. What time does the teacher's clock show right now? _____
   What was the time **eighty minutes** ago? _____

7. 100 more than 4907 = _____

8. Emma rolled a die **15** times. These are her results:
   6   5   5   6   3   1   2   4   4   1   6   5   5   5   6
   Which number was rolled **the least**? _____ Which number was rolled the **most**? _____

9. Which day of the week is 15th December? _____
   How many Wednesdays are there in December? _____
   What date is 3 days after Boxing Day?_____

10. There are 28 students in a class. 12 of them are girls.
    How many boys are there in the class? _____

10 Quick Questions a Day | www.lizardlearning.com

Name:	Date:	Year:

1. Rewrite this sentence with the correct **punctuation** and **spelling**:
   ava would you bring that to me pleese asked mrs aldred _____
   _____

2. **An adverb is a word which modifies or adds meaning to a verb, adjective or adverb by telling how, when or where a thing is done.** Write the **adverb/s** in this sentence:
   The children walked correctly across the road. _____

3. **Can you remember the meaning of contractions to complete this question?**
   Finish this sentence adding as many **contractions** as you can:
   He has not brought his swimming cap, _____

4. **Antonyms are words that are opposites.** Write an **antonym** for **true**: _____

5. **Rearrange** these words in **alphabetical** order: fifty / o'clock / fight / plant
   _____

6. What time does the teacher's clock show right now? _____
   Would it take **hours**, **minutes** or **seconds** to watch a movie? _____

7. Colour $\frac{1}{3}$ of these boxes: [| |]

8. 4 × ____ = 20   48 ÷ 6 = ____   ____ ÷ 7 = 4
   81 ÷ ____ = 9   ____ × 8 = 24   ____ ÷ 3 = 1
   6 × ____ = 42   14 ÷ ____ = 7   56 ÷ ____ = 8

9. Draw a **rectangular prism**:

10. 27 eggs were laid by 3 chickens.
    How many did they each lay?
    _____

Name: _____ Date: _____ Year: ____

1. Rewrite this sentence with the correct **punctuation** and **spelling**:
   did you knw dinosaurs had many bones in there bodys aded the museum scientist _____
   _____
   _____

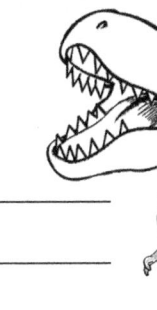

2. *A pronoun is a word that takes the place of a noun (e.g. her, him, it, themselves).*
   Write the **pronoun/s** in this sentence: _____
   Yesterday, she and I went to the shops to buy some groceries.

3. *Can you remember the meaning of plurals to complete this question?*
   Write two **plurals** in your **tidy box**: _____

4. *Can you remember the meaning of synonyms to complete this question?*
   Write a **synonym** for **fortunate**: _____

5. **Rearrange** these words in **alphabetical** order: clothes / coat / delighted / hammer
   _____

6. What time does the teacher's clock show right now? _____
   Write the digital form of **twenty minutes past 2**: [__ : __]

7. 10 × 4 = _____   7 × 2 = _____
   8 × 5 = _____   3 × 8 = _____

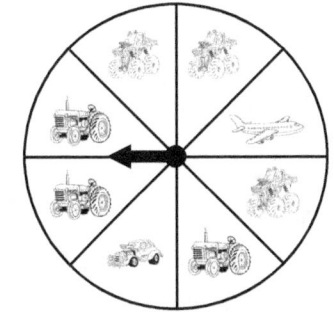

8. Is the spinner **least likely** to land on a tractor? _____
   Explain your answer: _____
   _____

9. Which of these objects has **more** capacity? _____

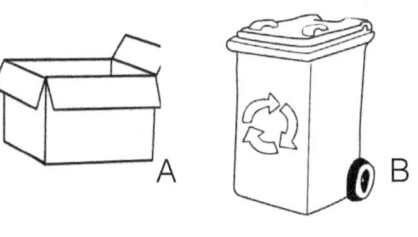

10. Five children each received 5 stickers for excellent work. How many stickers did the teacher have to give the children? _____

Year 4

Activity Pages: 44 – 53

Answers: 80 – 81

Name: _____ Date: _____ Year: _____

1. Rewrite the sentence/s with the correct **punctuation** and **spelling**:
   get out of my room jake kym screemed to her bruther every time he tryed entering her room
   _____
   _____

2. *A preposition is a word used before a noun or a pronoun to show its relationship to some other word in the sentence; it is used to make a phrase (e.g under the box, in the box, on the box, by, up, down, near, through, over, at).* Write the **preposition/s** you find in this phrase: inside the barn_____

3. *Plurals are words that mean more than one.*
   Write four singular words and have someone write their matching **plural**:
   _____ _____ _____ _____
   _____ _____ _____ _____

4. *Can you remember the meaning of antonyms to complete this question?* Write the definition of an **antonym**: _____
   _____
   _____

g	f	n	z	g
e	l	z	y	e
x	a	p	a	a
l	d	e	d	r
s	e	t	h	s
r	p	r	t	t
i	a	o	r	i
t	q	l	i	c
k	w	x	b	k

5. There are **three** words relating to **motoring**. There is one **odd** word which relates to a **celebration** once a year. Find all **four** words and write them on the lines below:
   _____
   _____
   _____

6. What time does the teacher's clock show right now? _____
   What will be the time **30 minutes** from now? _____
   Write the missing time: _____   9:20   9:50   10:20

7. What number are the **MAB blocks** showing? _____

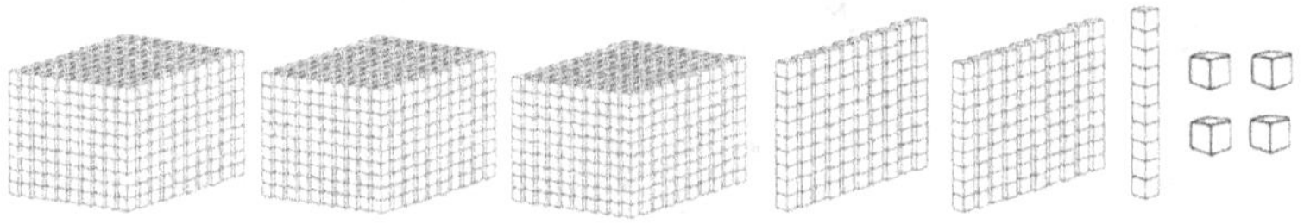

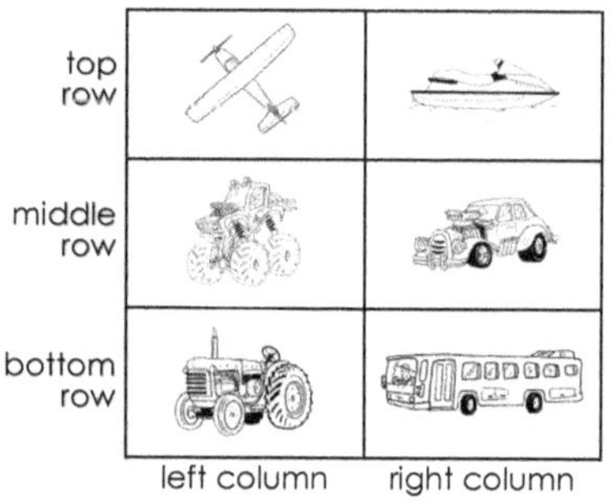

8. Write the mode of transport you see at position bottom row, left column: _____

   (top row; middle row; bottom row — left column, right column)

9. What **day** and **date** comes before 1 March this year? _____
   What **day** and **date** comes after 31 March? _____

10. Write an addition number story for the numbers 699 and 123: _____

Name: _____ Date: _____ Year: _____

1. Rewrite the sentence/s with the correct **punctuation** and **spelling**:
   maries father was a fireman at the local fire stachion _____
   _____

2. *A sentence or a clause, is a group of related words containing a subject and a verb.*
   Write one **clause** of your own: _____
   _____

3. *Compound words are two or more words joined together to form a new word (e.g. seashell).* Add a word to make a **compound** word:
   board _____ some _____ friend _____

4. *Synonyms are words that have similar meanings.*
   Write four words and ask someone to write **synonyms** for your words:
   _____ _____ _____ _____
   _____ _____ _____ _____

5. Write the **consonants** in the alphabet: _____
   _____

6. What time does the teacher's clock show right now? _____
   What was the time **35 minutes** ago? _____
   73 months + **59 months** = _____ Write the answer in **years** and **months**: _____

7. *Calculator Sentences - change 420 to 20 using your calculator (e.g. 420 – 400 = 20).*
   Write the **calculator sentence** you would need to change **396** to **96**: _____

8. What state is **north** of **Victoria**? _____

9. What **day/s** is Love You Forever being read? _____
   How **many** times is The Lion and the Mouse being read this week? _____

Reading Groups At The Local Library							
	9:15	**9:45**	**10:30**	**10:45**	**11:05**	**11:35**	**Noon**
Monday	Love you forever	Where the Wild Things Are	The Lorax	Guess How Much I Love You?	The Giving Tree	Harold and the Purple Crayon	Everyone Laughs
Wednesday	Everyone Laughs	Peek a Who	Green Eggs and Ham	The Very Hungry Caterpillar	Green Eggs and Ham	The Going to Bed Book	The Lorax
Thursday	The Lion and the Mouse	Press Here	Pat the Bunny	Goodnight Moon	The Lion and the Mouse	Press Here	The Lorax
Saturday	No David	No David	Pinkalicious	Moo Ba La La La	No David	Love you forever	Flotsam

10. Edmund bought a shirt for $42 and a pair of pants for $24.
    How much did he spend altogether? _____

1. Rewrite the sentence/s with the correct **punctuation** and **spelling**:
   the cows horses and chikens were locked away in there paddock and chiken coop at nite
   _____
   _____

2. **Contractions are shortened forms of two words.** Does this sentence use the **contraction** correctly? If not, rewrite the sentence correctly: They're books are in the bookcase.
   _____

3. **Plurals are words that mean more than one.** Write the **plurals** for:
   woman _____ teacher _____ uncle _____

4. **There are three articles: <u>the</u>, <u>a</u> and <u>an</u>. <u>The</u>,** is a definite article (e.g. give me the cup). **<u>A</u>,** is an indefinite article (e.g. give me a cup. This would be any cup). **<u>An</u>,** is the article to use before a vowel (e.g. an umbrella). Write the **article/s** in this sentence:
   The birds soared over the tree tops and down near a bird bath, beside an apple tree.
   _____

5. Write a word and then write the word in **future tense**: _____

6. What time does the teacher's clock show right now?_____
   What will be the time **40 minutes** from now?_____
   Eleven months - 2 months = _____

7. Write the **fraction** you see shaded: _____

8. Complete the pattern: $\frac{40}{100}$ $\frac{41}{100}$ $\frac{42}{100}$ ____ ____ ____ ____

9. How many **parallel lines** do you see? _____
   How many **right angles** do you see? _____

   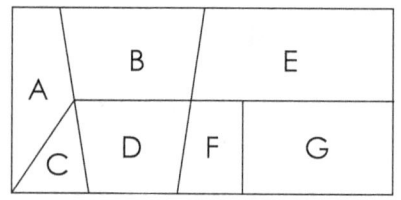

10. Complete this magic square so each row, column and diagonal adds to 72.

Name: _____ Date: _____ Year: _____

1. Rewrite the sentence/s with the correct **punctuation** and **spelling**:
   when you arive at a hotel the concierge takes youre bags from your car to youre room
   _____
   _____

2. Find and write the misspelled words in this sentence:
   The farrmer rownded up his cows for millking. _____

3. **Contractions are shortened forms of two words.**
   Write the long version of the **contractions** in this sentence: Let's go and play a fun game together and we'll have an ice-cream afterwards. _____

4. Write the **nearest meaning** to **sphere**: _____
   a) a round solid figure   **b)** a star does this in the night sky

5. **Rearrange** these words to make a proper sentence:
   bedroom goodnight was in my I a came book dad in when reading me. and said to _____
   _____
   _____

6. What time does the teacher's clock show right now? _____
   What will be the time **45 minutes** from now? _____
   Write the missing **12 hour times**:   10:55 _____   11:05   11:10 _____   11:20

7. I bought 12 chocolate bars for my birthday party.
   I handed over $30. How much change will I receive?
   _____

4 bars $8.00

8. Write the **number** for the tally marks shown in this table:

Tuckshop List	
Sandwich	𝍷𝍷𝍷𝍷𝍷 |||
Fruit	||
Chips	𝍷𝍷𝍷𝍷𝍷 𝍷𝍷𝍷𝍷𝍷 ||

9. **Area measures the size of a surface. Square centimetres is the measure used for small surfaces (e.g. the desk top). Square metres is used for larger surfaces (e.g. a football field). Formula for Area = Length x Width. 1cm² = 1cm x 1cm. A = L x W.**
   Find the **area** of this shape:
   _____ cm²

10. Sixteen giraffes had arrived at the zoo.
    The keepers had four pens for them to live in.
    How many giraffes in each pen? _____

Name: _____ Date: _____ Year: _____

1. Rewrite the sentence/s with the correct **punctuation** and **spelling**:
   thay realy didnt now what to do the storm was raging but all the anemals where still outside and where becomeing more disttresed _____
   _____

2. *Can you remember the meaning of pronouns to complete this question?*
   Write the definition of **pronouns**: _____
   _____

3. **Rearrange** this word. It relates to a **diamond ring**. Is the word a **Noun, verb** or **adjective**?
   glkisnpar _____ **noun, verb** or **adjective**? _____

4. *Can you remember the meaning of homographs and homophones to complete this question?*
   Write two separate sentences to explain these **homophones**:
   allowed: _____
   aloud: _____

5. *Writing Time!* Finish this sentence. We could not move the car as we… _____
   _____
   _____

6. What time does the teacher's clock show right now? _____
   What will be the time **50 minutes** from now? _____
   51 months + _____ months = **ninety-nine** months
   Write the answer above in **years** and **months**: _____ years _____ months

7. My answer is 12. I doubled the number and added 4. What number did I start with? _____
   Show your workings: _____

8.  x  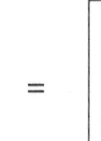 =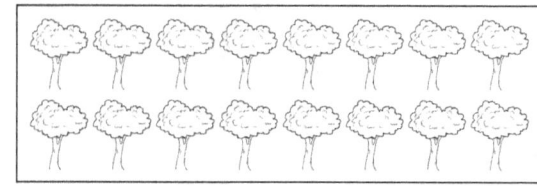

9. Place **L** or **mL** to match the label:

    250 ____    320 ____    750 ____    20 ____

10. Darcy had to lay telephone cable underground. 725 metres had to be placed in the ground first, but he only finished 616 metres before a storm came and he couldn't continue. How many more metres of cable are there left to be laid? _____

Name: _____   Date: _____   Year: _____

1. Rewrite the sentence/s with the correct **punctuation** and **spelling**:
   the soker team would practice every monday afternoon for there saturday game
   _____
   _____

2. Write the **dictionary** meaning for **drought**: _____
   _____

3. Correctly rewrite the mispelled words: crum / numba / memba / minute
   _____

4. **Synonyms are words that have similar meanings.**
   Think of four **synonyms**. *Test someone on their knowledge of synonyms that would match!*
   _____
   _____ _____ _____ _____

5. Write the words you find in this word worm: _____

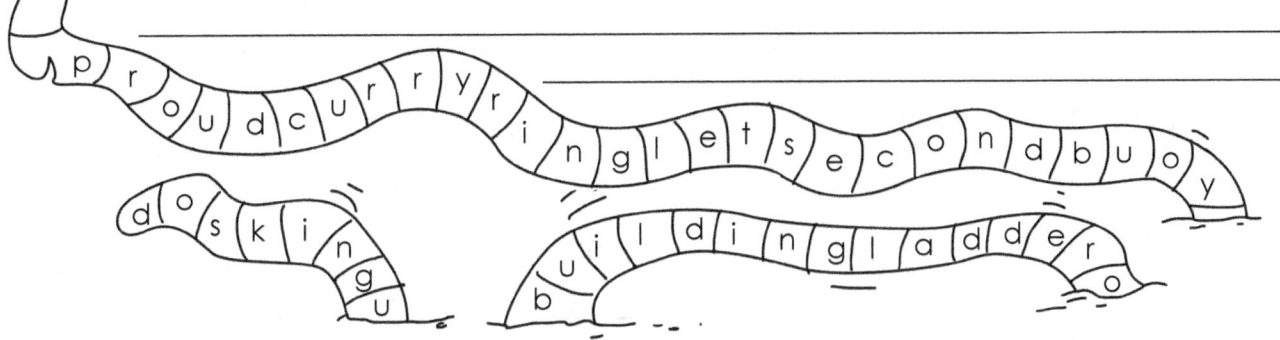

6. What time does the teacher's clock show right now? _____
   What will be the time **15 minutes** from now? _____
   What is the missing **24 hour** time?   15:15   15:10   15:05   15:00   _____

7. Write the **calculator sentence** to change **6 178** to **5 995** = _____

8. Write the states that are **south** of **Queensland**:
   _____

9. Would you use **L** or **mL** to measure the following?
   A jam jar: _____   A bathtub: _____

10. Write a subtraction number story for 613 and 599:
    _____
    _____

10 Quick Questions a Day | www.lizardlearning.com

Name: _____ Date: _____ Year: _____

1. Rewrite the sentence/s with the correct **punctuation** and **spelling**:
   giants are not just foand in farytale stories and myths in fact in turkey ther is a man who is more than 2 and a half meters tall _____
   _____
   _____

2. **Can you remember the meaning of prepositions to complete this question?**
   Write the definition of **prepositions**: _____
   _____

3. **Jumble** four spelling words from your weekly class list. *Test someone to see if they can work out your challenge!* _____
   _____

4. **Homophones are two or more words that sound the same but have different meanings or spellings (e.g. right / write).** Write two separate sentences for these **homophones**:
   wear: _____
   where: _____

5. Write four words that have three **vowels** in them: _____
   _____

6. What time does the teacher's clock show right now? _____
   What was the time **55 minutes** ago? _____
   What are the missing **24 hour** times?   15:10 _____   15:30 _____   15:50

7. **True** or **false**?   5 x 5 equals twenty-five _____   36 ÷ 6 = 4 _____

8. Complete:

   $3\overline{)9}$ $\overline{)72}^{9}$ $8\overline{)}^{4}$ $\overline{)99}^{9}$ $7\overline{)77}$ $\overline{)108}^{12}$ $9\overline{)63}$

9. **Converting Litres (L) to millilitres (mL) x 1000.**
   Converting millilitres (mL) to Litres (L) ÷ 1000.
   Convert these measurements from **mL** to **L**:
   9 000 mL _____   7 000mL _____
   4 500mL _____   1 264mL _____

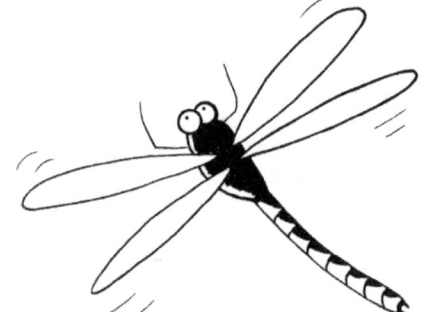

10. Julian had 385 eggs delivered but 96 were cracked in transport.
    How many eggs are left now? _____

Name: _____ Date: _____ Year: _____

1. Rewrite the sentence/s with the correct **punctuation** and **spelling**:
   i arsked my grandmuver when she was borne she said 1943
   _____
   _____

2. *Can you remember the meaning of nouns to complete this question?*
   Write whether the following words are **proper nouns** or **common nouns**:
   octopus _____ elephant _____
   Monday _____ roses _____

3. *Plurals are words that mean more than one.*
   Write out four singular words and have someone write their matching **plural**:
   _____ _____ _____ _____
   _____ _____ _____ _____

4. *Can you remember the meaning of articles to complete this question?*
   Write the definition of **articles**: _____
   _____

5. **Rearrange** these words in **alphabetical** order: _____
   _____

   plumber   quadrilateral   October   fifth   quotient   oblong

6. What time does the teacher's clock show right now? _____
   What will be the time **10 minutes** from now? _____
   74 months + 60 months = _____   **How many** _____ years _____ months?

7. Write the **fraction** shaded: a) _____ b) _____
   a) [bar divided into 5 parts, 1 shaded]   b) [bar divided into 7 parts, 6 shaded]

8. Which series of numbers show **counting backwards** in **4's**? _____
   a) 25, 20, 15, 10   b) 80, 76, 72, 68   c) 50, 40, 20, 10   d) 100, 200, 300, 400

9. *Converting kilograms (kg) to grams (g) × 1000.*
   Converting grams (g) to kilograms (kg) ÷ 1000.
   Convert: **6 000 grams** to kilograms: _____   **4.213 kilograms** to grams: _____

10. Parents left 36 cakes in the staffroom. Today, nine teachers came into the staff room and ate every cake on the table. How many cakes each did the teachers receive? _____
    Show your workings: _____

10 Quick Questions a Day | www.lizardlearning.com

| Name: | Date: | Year: |

1. Rewrite the sentence/s with the correct **punctuation** and **spelling**:
   bamboo is one of the fastist groing plants the gardener was telling her customa
   _____

2. *An adverb is a word which modifies or adds meaning to a verb, adjective or adverb by telling how, when or where a thing is done.* Write a sentence using one **adverb**: _____
   _____

3. *Can you remember the meaning of prefixes to complete this question?*
   Correctly add a **prefix** -re, -in or -im to **think**: _____

4. *There are three articles: the, a and an. The, is a definite article (e.g. give me the cup). A, is an indefinite article (e.g. give me a cup. This would be any cup). An, is the article to use before a vowel (e.g. an umbrella).* Write the **article/s** in this sentence:
   The weather was so cold I wore a beanie on my head. _____

5. *Writing Time!* Finish this sentence: The crocodile was very angry… _____
   _____
   _____

6. What time does the teacher's clock show right now?_____
   What will be the time **30 minutes** from now? _____
   _____ months + 22 months = ninety-three months

7. This recipe makes 6 iceblocks. There are 18 children in the class. Change the amounts so we make 18 iceblocks:

   $\frac{2}{3}$ cup orange juice   _____ cups orange juice
   $\frac{1}{4}$ cup frozen raspberries   _____ cup frozen raspberries
   $\frac{1}{4}$ cup frozen blueberries   _____ cup frozen blueberries
   6 strawberries, halved   _____ strawberries, halved

8. Complete the **pattern**:

    _____    _____ _____ _____

9. **Converting Litres (L) to millilitres (mL) x 1000. Converting millilitres (mL) to Litres (L) ÷ 1000.** *Challenge!* **Convert** these measurements to **mL**:
   $7\frac{1}{2}$ L _____ $4\frac{1}{2}$ L _____ $5\frac{1}{2}$ L _____   *Challenge!* 1 362 L _____

10. The secretary had 24 thumbtacks to pin notes to the notice board.
    Each corner had a thumbtack. How many notes did she have? _____

| Name: | Date: | Year: |

1. Rewrite the sentence/s with the correct **punctuation** and **spelling**:
   look at that raynbow it has beatiful colors noticed danielle _____
   _____

2. **Adjectives are describing words.** Write the **strongest adjective** from this list:
   crashing / breaking / smashing / shattering _____

3. **Rearrange** these words. The words in the box are spelled out correctly to help you:
   ficultifd _____ gealliv _____ | umpire | village |
   qiliud _____ preimu _____ | difficult | liquid |

4. **Can you remember the meaning of homographs and homophones to complete this question?** Is the word **strait** in this sentence a **homograph** or **homophone**? _____
   Bass Strait is the body of water between Victoria and Tasmania.

5. **Writing Time!** Finish this sentence: When I closed the gate I closed it on my… _____
   _____
   _____

6. What time does the teacher's clock show right now? _____
   What will be the time **20 minutes** from now? _____
   What is the missing **24 hour** time?   _____   17:41   17:38   17:35   17:32

7. Write out the 5 x tables. Write the **turnaround** beside. Here is an example to start you off:
   First way: *The turnaround way:*
   0 x 5 = 0   _____   0 ÷ 5 = 0   _____
   1 x 5 = 5   _____   5 ÷ 5 = 1   _____
   _____ _____   _____ _____
   _____ _____   _____ _____
   _____ _____   _____ _____

8. Complete:
   3)12̄   54)9̄   7)8̄   63)9̄   9)1̄1̄08   5)9̄

9. **Converting kilograms (kg) to grams (g) x 1000. Converting grams (g) to kilograms (kg) ÷ 1000.** Convert: **8 kilograms** to grams _____   **4.5 kilograms** to grams _____

10. The landscaper was hired to lay the turf around the motel. On the first day he laid 873 metres. He had 1 385 to lay altogether. How many metres did he have to lay on the second day?
    _____ *Show your workings:* _____

Year 5

Activity Pages: 56 – 65
Answers: 81 – 82

Name: _____ Date: _____ Year: _____

1. Rewrite the sentence/s with the correct **punctuation** and **spelling**:
   ms pottss lunches were alwayz yummy
   _____

2. **Can you remember the meaning of phrases to complete this question?**
   Write a sentence that contains a **phrase**:_____
   _____

3. **Compound words are two or more words joined together to f0rm a new word (e.g. seashell).**
   Write a **compound** word you would find in the classroom:_____

4. **Homophones are two or more words that sound the same but have different meanings or spellings (e.g. right / write).** Write the correct **homophone** in this sentence:
   He went to the student council meeting to _____ (rays / maze / raise)
   a few important issues.

5. Write the five **vowels**: _____

6. What time does the teacher's clock show right now?_____
   What was the time **fifteen hours** ago? _____
   19 months = _____ year _____ months

7. Write out the 8 x tables. Write the **division facts** beside. Here is an example to start you off:
   0 x 8 = 0   _____   0 ÷ 8 = 0   _____
   1 x 8 = 8   _____   8 ÷ 8 = 1   _____
   _____   _____   _____   _____
   _____   _____   _____   _____
   _____   _____   _____   _____

8. **< means less than > means greater than**
   three hundred and forty-three ☐ 354   9.54 ☐ 9½ $7.50 ☐ seven and three quarters

9. **Draw** the translation of this picture:

10. 5 friends decided they would combine their money to buy as many packets of potato chips for the end of year party as they could. They had $5 each and a packet of chips is $2.
    How many packets can they afford? _____

Name: _____ Date: _____ Year: _____

1. Rewrite the sentence/s with the correct **punctuation** and **spelling**:
   ian could neva rememeber if the postcode for his howse was 3058 or 3057 which one is it he asked his mum _____
   _____

2. Write the **dictionary** meaning for **astonishment**: _____
   _____

3. *Contractions are shortened forms of two words.*
   Does this sentence use the **contraction** correctly? _____
   Spelling is one of my weaknesses, but it's one of you're strengths.

4. **Can you remember the meaning of homographs to complete this question?**
   Provide one example of a **homograph** in a **kitchen**: _____

5. Write five words. Make one the **odd** one out. *Test someone near you.*
   _____

6. What time does the teacher's clock show right now? _____
   What was the time **15 hours and 15 minutes** ago? _____

7. Round these numbers to the nearest **100**:
   899 _____ 273 _____ 398 _____ 999 _____ 3 198 _____

8. Using the words **least likely** and **most likely,** answer these questions on the line provided:
   That it will rain today: _____
   That your principal will be wearing his swimmers to parade on Friday: _____
   That you will have two lunch breaks to play today: _____

9. **Area measures the size of a surface. Square centimetres is the measure used for small surfaces (e.g. the desk top). Square metres is used for larger surfaces (e.g. a football field). Formula for Area = Length x Width. 1cm² = 1cm x 1cm. A = L x W.**
   Which is the correct **area** for this rectangle?
   _____
   12cm² / 27cm² / 36cm²

   9cm
   3cm [rectangle]

10. Their dad withdrew $60 out of the ATM before he drove to the petrol station. When there he spent $35 on petrol; $2 on a newspaper; $2.80 on milk and $3.60 on a loaf of bread. How much was remaining of the $60? _____

Name: _____ Date: _____ Year: _____

1. Rewrite the sentence/s with the correct **punctuation** and **spelling**:
   ive neva understand how if the earths round and always turning we dont fall of i realise its because of gravity but im still not sure how it works _____
   _____
   _____

2. *Proper nouns are the actual names of people, places, animals or things.*
   Write whether the following words are **proper nouns** or **common nouns**:
   fish paste _____ water _____ Sydney _____ Japan _____
   house _____ Max _____ Little Miss Muffet _____ St James _____

3. Find and write the **misspelled** words in this sentence: _____
   Next weak I am going on a holaday with my famalee.

4. *Can you remember the meaning of antonyms to complete this question?*
   Write the definition of **antonyms**: _____
   _____

5. **Rearrange** the words to make this sentence make sense:
   were in the park fell children broke when The one arm. playing of them and his _____
   _____

6. What time does the teacher's clock show right now? _____
   What was the time **15 hours and 26 minutes** ago? _____
   Write **five past two** in digital time: ☐ : ☐

7. Write the **smaller** number: 3 930 829   3 392 039 _____

8. Name a person or object that is sitting **south east** of you: _____
   Name a person or object that is sitting **south west** of you: _____

9. *Area measures the size of a surface. Square centimetres is the measure used for small surfaces (e.g. the desk top). Square metres is used for larger surfaces (e.g. a football field). Formula for Area = Length x Width. 1cm^2 = 1cm x 1cm. A = L x W.*
   True or **false**? Every **face** on a cube is a square? _____
   Every **face** on the diagram has an area of **12cm^2**? _____

10. Trixie had $10 pocket money, but owed her brother $4.50.
    Will she have enough money to buy a $5.90 pair of earrings?
    _____

3cm

10 Quick Questions a Day | www.lizardlearning.com

Name: _____ Date: _____ Year: _____

1. Rewrite the sentence/s with the correct **punctuation** and **spelling**:
   apples 99 cents a kilo of oranges 399 they could here the fruiterer calling out his bargan speschals from the topp end of the shopping center _____
   _____
   _____

2. **Verbs are doing / action words.** Identify the **verb** in this sentence:
   In the morning my friends will be swimming. _____

3. This word is jumbled. It involves **mass**. What is the word and is it a **noun**, **verb** or **adjective**?
   gmakloirs _____

4. Write the definition of **synonyms**: _____
   _____

5. **Writing Time!** Finish this sentence: The camp fire was burning nicely but sparks were flying everywhere and then... _____
   _____

6. What time does the teacher's clock show right now? _____
   What will be the time **15 and ½ hours** from now? _____

7. **Calculator Sentences** - change 420 to 20 using your calculator (e.g. 420 – 400 = 20).
   Write one **calculator sentence** you could use to change:
   5 428 to **428** = _____

8. At which **coordinates** are Perth and Hobart?
   _____
   How many states are in **4C**? _____

9. Write the missing angle on this straight angle:

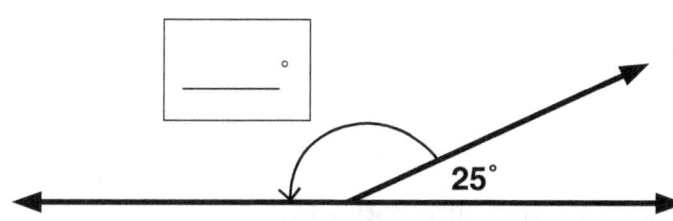

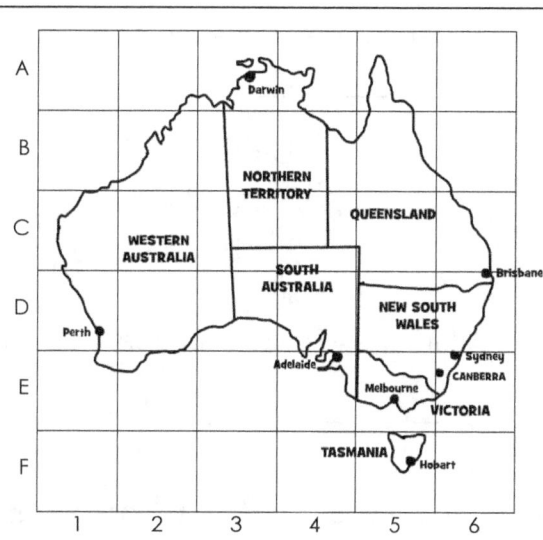

10. April had a very long pony-tail that measured 36cm. Unfortunately she got some chewing gum stuck in her hair and had to get 140mm cut off along with the gum. How long was her ponytail after her accident, in millimetres? _____ mm

10 Quick Questions a Day | www.lizardlearning.com

1. Rewrite the sentence/s with the correct **punctuation** and **spelling**:
   the netball coach wasnt happy with cindy when she mist the net again because she knew cindy wasnt trying come on she called from across the court _____
   _____
   _____

2. *Can you remember the meaning of prepositions to complete this question?*
   Write the **preposition/s** in this sentence: _____
   The child threw his food onto the floor and was then in trouble for being naughty.

3. Find the **misspelled** words in this sentence and write them correctly: Won day we will be abel to traval far accross the univerce. _____

4. *Can you remember the meaning of articles to complete this question?*
   List the **article/s** in this sentence: _____
   "I'm wanting to see an emu today Mummy," said the excited little girl at the zoo visit.

5. Write five words. Make one the **odd** one out. *Test someone near you.*
   _____
   _____

6. What time does the teacher's clock show right now?_____
   What will be the time **19 hours** from now? _____
   831 days = _____ weeks _____ days

7. What number does the **abacus** show?
   _____

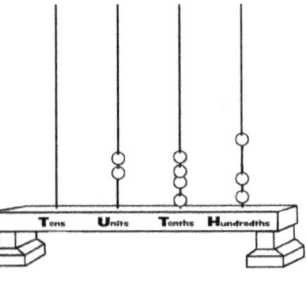

8. Write these mixed numbers as **improper fractions** (e.g. $3\frac{8}{10} = \frac{7}{2}$)

   $2\frac{1}{4} =$ _____ $4\frac{1}{5} =$ _____ $2\frac{3}{4} =$ _____ $7\frac{1}{2} =$ _____ $2\frac{2}{5} =$ _____

9. Would you use **cm²**, **m²** or **hectares** to measure a **dining room table**? _____

10. Remy was 1.5m tall. However, when he put on shoes, it added 20mm to his height. How tall in metres and centimetres, was Remy with his shoes on? _____

Name: _____ Date: _____ Year: _____

1. Rewrite the sentence/s with the correct **punctuation** and **spelling**:
   the gold fish in the pound liked two blow bubles when u walk parst them they look up at u from the warter i think they r waiting four fewd _____
   _____
   _____

2. *Can you remember the meaning of verbs to complete this question?*
   Write the **verbs** in this sentence: She wanted to go shopping for some new shoes as her old shoes broke. _____

3. *Compound words are two or more words joined together to form a new word (e.g. seashell).* Complete these **compound** words:
   chain_____   rain_____   _____stool

4. Which definition best describes **conductor**: _____
   a) A person who directs the performance of an orchestra or choir.
   b) Another name for a unit of measurement in math.

5. There are **three** words relating to a **nasty character**.
   There is one **odd** word which relates to the **garden**.
   Find all **four** words and write them on the lines below:
   _____
   _____
   _____

r	r	m	s	p
d	e	o	r	o
l	t	n	e	r
i	s	s	w	e
v	i	t	o	v
e	n	e	l	u
s	i	r	f	j
e	s	n	f	g
r	r	v	s	r

6. What time does the teacher's clock show right now? _____
   What was the time **21 hours and 19 minutes** ago? _____

7. Underline the **largest** number: 1 483 848 / 1 483 231

8. What was the **difference** in weight from when the baby was born to when it was 5 months old?
   _____
   What was the baby's **approximate weight** in December? _____

9. **Re-draw** this 2D shape as a **3D** shape:

10. A room in Lana's house has an area of 12m^2.
    List 2 possible combinations of length and width for the room. _____

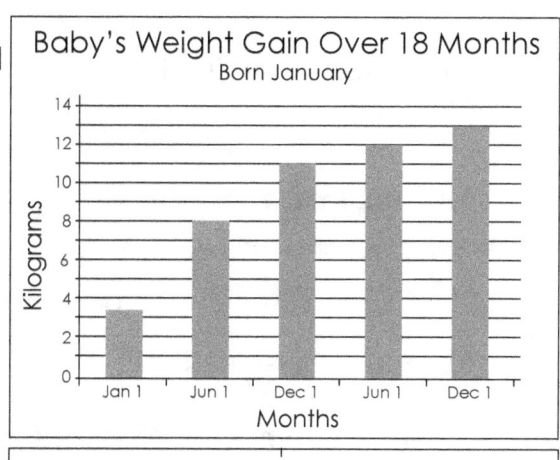

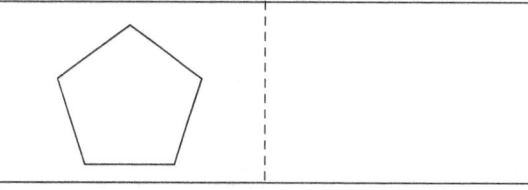

| Name: | Date: | Year: |

1. Rewrite the sentence/s with the correct **punctuation** and **spelling**:
   each morning at shift changover the nurses stachion was full of speshialists physiotherapusts nutritionists and of corse nurses it was important that each person was their at 7am to discuss the patience progress from the night befoure _____
   _____
   _____
   _____
   _____

2. **Can you remember the meaning of nouns to complete this question?**
   Write whether these words are **proper nouns** or **common nouns**:
   walk _____ dog _____ Steep Hill Road _____
   James _____ street _____ Brisbane _____

3. **A suffix is a letter or group of letters placed after or at the end of a word to change its meaning.** Which word would make sense if both **suffixes** -ly and -er are used:
   correct / loud / fall _____

4. **Can you remember the meaning of antonyms to complete this question?**
   Write the definition of **antonyms**: _____

5. **Writing Time!** Finish this sentence: The farmer was milking the cow when the bucket ...
   _____
   _____

6. What time does the teacher's clock show right now? _____
   What was the time **19 hours 45 minutes** ago? _____

7. Complete this **decimal pattern**:
   0.7   0.6   0.5   _____ _____ _____ _____ _____

8. < means less than   > means greater than   = equal to
   one thousand and eighty-nine ☐ 1 890   0.64 ☐ $\frac{46}{100}$ 4.73 ☐ $4\frac{3}{4}$
   $17.48 ☐ seventeen and a half
   48 392 ☐ forty-eight thousand, three hundred and twenty-nine

9. Convert **12.14m** to **centimetres**: _____ Convert **3.6m** to **mm**: _____

10. When joined together George's power cords are 8.4m long, if George has 4 power cords how long is each cord? _____

10 Quick Questions a Day | www.lizardlearning.com

Name: _____ Date: _____ Year: _____

1. Rewrite the sentence/s with the correct **punctuation** and **spelling**:
   it had been raning four days and paula wundered when it would stop she wanted to ride her bike from aspley to caboolture but wasnt about to do that hole cerkut in a down poor of rane _____
   _____
   _____

2. **Verbs are doing / action words.** Write five **verbs** that apply to a **hairdresser**: _____
   _____

3. **Plurals are words that mean more than one.** Make these words **plural**: toe _____
   planet _____ photo _____
   change _____ canvas _____

4. **Can you remember the meaning of antonyms to complete this question?**
   Write **antonyms** for: friend _____ easy _____ careful _____
   warm _____ allowed _____ disagree _____ healthy _____

5. Rewrite these words in **alphabetical** order: _____
   _____

   oblique   swarm   perimeter   overboard   ache

6. What time does the teacher's clock show right now? _____
   What will be the time **20 hours** from now? _____
   Write the time **12 hours before 6:05am** on the clock face:

   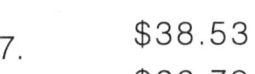

7. $38.53 $41.25 $17.03 $12.46
   + $26.79   - $37.77   x   4   x   8
   _____   _____   _____   _____

   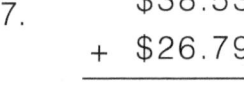

8. Which country is **north** of Australia? _____
   Name the sea that is **north** of the Northern Territory: _____

9. **Formula for the perimeter of a rectangle L = length, W = width, and P = perimeter.**
   P = L + L + W + W or P = 2 x L + 2 x W or P = 2 x (L + W).
   Find the **perimeter** of this **rectangle**:
   P = _____

   11cm, 4cm

10. The water on the stove is boiling, which means it is 100°C. It needs to cool down to 65°C for the food Sally is cooking.
    How much does the temperature need to drop by? _____

| Name: | Date: | Year: |

1. Rewrite the sentence/s with the correct **punctuation** and **spelling**:
   thats gross yelled sonia at dominika dominika had tricked her sonya hadnt realised the lolly that she had given her was very very sour instead of sweet _____
   _____
   _____

2. *Adjectives are describing words.* Write the **strongest adjective** from this list:
   weary / tired / sleepy / exhausted / lethargic _____

3. *Compound words are two or more words joined together to form a new word (e.g. seashell).* Write a **compound** word in the **bathroom**: _____

4. *Can you remember the meaning of synonyms to complete this question?*
   Write the definition of **synonyms**: _____

5. Write the words you find in this word worm: _____
   _____
   _____

   (word worm containing letters: information, index, symmetry, yards, astonish, equipment, eight, ok)

6. What time does the teacher's clock show right now?_____
   What will be the time **20 hours and 13 minutes** from now?_____
   How many minutes between **9:55am** and **10:23am**? _____ minutes

7. Write the **value** of the highlighted digit in this number: 1 372 83**9** _____

8. Create your own **number pattern** on the number line using jumps, then write the **rule**:

   |____|____|____|____|____|____|____|____|____|____|

   The **rule** is: _____

9. **Converting kilograms (kg) to grams (g) x 1000. Converting grams (g) to kilograms (kg) ÷ 1000.** Convert **6 019 grams** to **kilograms**: _____

10. Sam wanted the heater to warm his room up to a temperature equal to 3 x 7.
    What temperature did he want the room to be? _____

10 Quick Questions a Day | www.lizardlearning.com

Name: _____ Date: _____ Year: _____

1. Rewrite the sentence/s with the correct **punctuation** and **spelling**:
on the televishion moniters at the space staytion a red spot beecame visible on the satelite system it appeered too the astronawts that there may be an alien spacecraft nearbye on closer look it was just a speck of dust _____
_____
_____
_____

2. *Can you remember the meaning of pronouns to complete this question?*
Write the definition of **pronouns**: _____

3. Which words out of this list are spelled incorrectly? Spell the incorrect ones properly: ____
_____
_____

confuse, believe, ajust, frite, frustration, frends, location, staton, draw, shelf

4. Write a word that has the nearest meaning to **patience**: _____

5. Write five words that have four **vowels** in them. *You could use your dictionary to help you:*
_____
_____

6. What time does the teacher's clock show right now?_____
What was the time **20 hours and 20 minutes** ago? _____
How many years in **half a century**? _____ years

7. If there are 80 dogs at the park, how many are Bull Dogs?_____

Dogs at the Park
A Golden Retriever 25%
B Rottweiler 15%
C Fox Terrier 25%
D Bull Dog 35%

8. = **equal to** or ≠ **not equal to**
38 492 ☐ 38 000 + 492
one thousand, four hundred and sixty ☐ 146
285 ☐ two hundred and eighty-five
$1.50 ☐ $0.50 $0.50 $0.10 $0.10 $0.05

9. What **3D** shape does a hose make? _____

10. George is making biscuits. He uses 230g of flour, 120g of butter, 90g of sugar and 100g of chocolate chips. What is the total weight of his mixture? _____

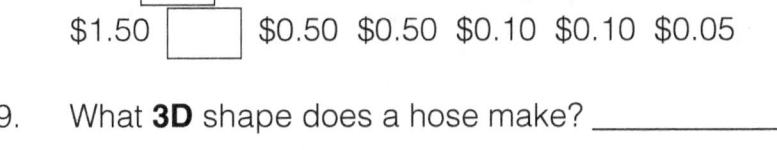

Year 6

Activity Pages: 68 – 77
Answers: 82 – 83

Name: _____ Date: _____ Year: _____

1. Rewrite the sentence/s with the correct **punctuation** and **spelling**:
   her baby was 3 yers old and she so badley wanted her doorter too be bapetised at the local church the mother finalley found a wonderfull church cawled st johns church the preests name was father thomas shepard who wellcomed the to lovingly into his church
   _____
   _____
   _____
   _____

2. *A phrase is a group of words without a verb. Many phrases start with a preposition.*
   Write a sentence that contains two **phrases**: _____
   _____

3. *Compound words are two or more words joined together to form a new word (e.g. seashell).* Write a sentence that includes two **compound** words:
   _____
   _____

4. *Can you remember the meaning of synonyms to complete this question?*
   Think of six words. *Test someone on their knowledge of **synonyms** that would match!*
   _____

5. Circle the **ellipsis** in the box: | ; | : | ? | ... | , |

6. What time does the teacher's clock show right now? _____
   What will be the time **seventy-five hours and thirty-three minutes** from now? _____
   50 years = _____ decades

7. 52 - 48 ÷ 4 = _____   15 + 28 ÷ 4 = _____

8. Draw a **bar graph** to match the information given:

Classroom Hair Colour	
Brown	13
Black	3
Blonde	6
Red	1

9. Convert this time to **12 hour (am/pm)** time **15:15**: _____

10. 11 school students each had 3 sandwiches to eat for the day. How many sandwiches, during the week, did they have between them? _____

| Name: | Date: | Year: |

1. Rewrite the sentence/s with the correct **punctuation** and **spelling**:
   get out mavis screemed at the dirty dog who was walking mud thru the house _____
   _____

2. Write the **dictionary** meaning for **elaborate**: _____
   _____

3. *Can you remember the meaning of contractions to complete this question?*
   Write the definition of **contractions**: _____
   _____

4. *The article an goes before vowels. The article a goes before consonants. The article the goes before nouns (e.g. the table, a dog, an umbrella).*
   Write **definite** or **indefinite articles** to complete this sentence: _____ overpass was being built so that traffic could travel more quickly into _____ city.

5. There are **three** words relating to the **flavours** of food. There is **one** odd word which is the **ingredient** that gives chocolate its taste. Find and write all **four** words:
   _____
   _____

p	t	e	n	n
c	a	l	e	s
t	n	e	k	a
d	g	c	c	l
g	y	t	o	t
s	p	i	c	y
t	u	e	o	r
e	n	r	a	m

6. What time does the teacher's clock show right now? _____
   What will be the time **62 hours and 10 minutes** from now?
   _____
   Emelyn was born in **2008**. How old will she be in **2064**? _____

7. Write the **factors** of **48**: _____

8. Complete the **counting pattern**. Determine the rule *(you may use a calculator)*:
   Challenge!   1   8   27   64   _____ _____ _____ _____ _____
   Rule: _____

9. *Area measures the size of a surface. Square centimetres is the measure used for small surfaces (e.g. the desk top). Square metres is used for larger surfaces (e.g. a football field). Formula for Area = Length x Width. 1cm² = 1cm x 1cm. A = L x W.*
   Write the correct **area** based on the measurements given: **length 4cm width 17cm**
   68cm²   86cm²   58cm²   _____

10. 6 friends had all put equal amounts of money towards buying a new computer game. The game cost $108; how much did each person contribute? _____

10 Quick Questions a Day | www.lizardlearning.com

Name: _____   **Date:** _____   **Year:** _____

1. Rewrite the sentence/s with the correct **punctuation** and **spelling**:
   the too horses where locked away in the stabels untill the storm cleared the stabels assistant was constently talking two the horses calmely saying theyre their its alrght boys the thundar and lightning will stop soone and then you can galop around the medows again _____
   _____
   _____
   _____

2. *Conjunctions are joining words used to connect words, phrases, clauses or sentences. The conjunction may be used at the beginning of a sentence as well as within (e.g. John went into the shop but he forgot to buy bread. Although John went into the shop, he forgot to buy bread).* Write the **conjunction** in the sentence: _____
   I had just fed the dog, yet he stole some of my chips off my plate when I wasn't looking.

3. Locate the incorrectly spelled words. Write them correctly:
   overwhelm / equavalent / quotation / lingiust _____

4. *Can you remember the meaning of similes to complete this question?*
   Finish this sentence with a **simile**: The ocean was… _____
   _____

5. Write six words that have five **vowels** in them: _____
   _____

6. What time does the teacher's clock show right now? _____
   What will be the time **12 hours and fifty-nine minutes** from now? _____
   six hundred and sixty-nine minutes = _____ hours _____ minutes

7. Write the **value** of 4 in **43 731 295**: _____

8. **Tally** this information:

Cars in the Car Park		Tally Marks
Blue	13	
White	24	
Red	28	
Silver	22	
Green	14	
Yellow	4	
Black	11	

9. Write the most appropriate measurement **cm³** / **m³** to measure a **shoe box**: _____

10. Their aunt who was visiting them from Germany had $150 that she intended to share between her beloved nieces. She wanted to give each of her 4 nieces $30 and buy a cake for dessert hat evening. How much can she spend on the cake? _____

Name: _____ Date: _____ Year: _____

1. Rewrite the sentence/s with the correct **punctuation** and **spelling**:
   the chilldren demonstreted encredible iniative in righting a play entitled adopt a pet
   _____
   _____

2. *Colloquialism is an informal phrase common in everyday speech that is often specific to a country or area (e.g. bonza, crikey, g'day, Aussie, bloke).*
   Write your own sentence that includes the following **colloquialisms**: mutt rad
   _____

3. **Rearrange** six spelling words from your weekly class list. *Test someone to see if they can work out your challenge!* _____
   _____

4. Write the word with the **nearest meaning** to **forward**: ahead / front / move _____

5. Write the missing **tenses** in the table:

Past	Present	Future
	hate	
	negotiate	
		will mourn
fixed		
	type	
		will/shall yell

6. What time does the teacher's clock show right now? _____
   What was the time **eighty-seven hours and six minutes** ago? _____
   63 days = _____ weeks _____ days

7. *Calculator Sentences* - Change 420 to 20 using your calculator (e.g. 420 – 400 = 20).
   Write two different **calculator sentences** to change the number from **738** to **200**:
   _____

8. = equal to or ≠ not equal to $\frac{3}{8}$ ☐ 0.375 $\frac{3}{4}$ ☐ 0.75 $\frac{1}{2}$ ☐ 0.25

9. *Volume is length x width x height. V = L x W x H. The symbol for cubic centimetres is abbreviated as cm³ (e.g. 3cm x 2cm x 7cm = 42cm³).*
   How many **cubic metres** are in this **rectangular prism**?
   _____

   7m, 6m, 9m

10. Mike is 8, his sister Jenny is 6 and his brother John is 10. What is their average age? _____

1. Rewrite the sentence/s with the correct **punctuation** and **spelling**:
   the fotografers job at a weding can be very stresful the event happens only once and the fotografer needs to be able to capture all the brides and grooms most significant moments in a skillful and artistic way _____
   _____
   _____
   _____

2. *Adverbs are words that modify a verb, adjective or adverb.* Write a sentence using two **adverbs**: _____
   _____

3. *Can you remember the meaning of compound words to complete this question?*
   Write a **compound** word you would find at a **high school**: _____

4. *Synonyms are words that have similar meanings.* Write a **synonym** to these six words:
   enchanted _____ swathe _____ traverse _____
   compound _____ foundation _____ endurance _____

5. Which sentence below is a **rhetorical question**: _____
   a) Is he the grumpiest cat in the world?   b) Is your cat very grumpy?

6. What time does the teacher's clock show right now? _____
   What will be the time **38 hours and 55 minutes** from now? _____
   What **fraction** of a century is **4 years**? Write in lowest terms: _____

7. How much money is shown? _____

8. 18 ÷ (_____ x _____) = 6   24 ÷ (_____ ÷ _____) = 6   20 = 12 + (_____ ÷ _____)

9. Draw the **top** view and **front** view of this **3D** shape:
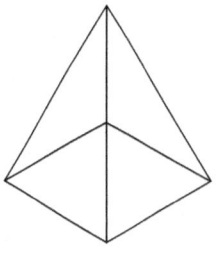

10. Earl needs to get his new bookshelf through the door to his study. The door is 75.2cm wide, the bookshelf is 48.5cm wide. How much room will he have either side of the bookshelf when he is moving it? _____

Name: _____ Date: _____ Year: _____

1. Rewrite the sentence/s with the correct **punctuation** and **spelling**:
   lila was wachting a dockumentory on cheetahs shed nevar seen an animil mooove so fast it was incredable she told her mom that cheetas were in facted the farstest animils on earth also the best lorking whatss that saying farster then the spead of lite she comented
   _____
   _____
   _____
   _____

2. **Adjectives are describing words.** Write six examples of an **adjective**:
   _____
   _____

3. **Rearrange** these words. The words in the box are spelled correctly to help you.
   catiotmua _____   suapllebi _____ | plausible   mournful
   fulnmour _____   notirpecua _____ | precaution   automatic

4. Write the word with the **nearest meaning** to **failure**: crash / malfunction / loser
   _____

5. **Rearrange** these words to make a proper sentence: to remember the steps It is sometimes difficult involved in on the computer. opening up a new document _____
   _____
   _____

6. What time does the teacher's clock show right now? _____
   What was the time **20 and a quarter hours** ago? _____
   Write **45 minutes past four** in digital time:

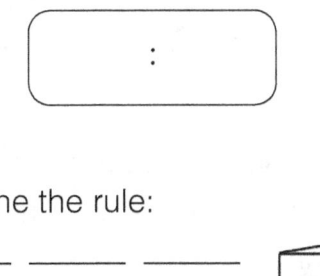

7. Show **9 163** on the **abacus**:

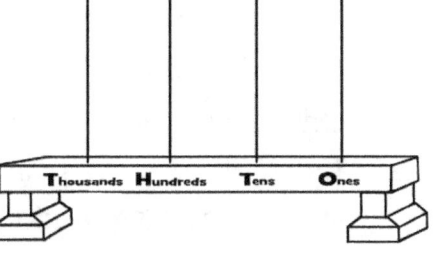

8. Complete the **counting pattern.** Determine the rule:
   12   15   18   21   ___ ___ ___ ___ ___
   Rule: _____

9. Write the best unit to **measure** the length of a **swimming pool**: _____

10. Christine used $\frac{12}{15}$ of her textas in the first week of school.
    What fraction of her textas hasn't she used? _____
    Write as a fraction in lowest terms, decimal and a percentage: _____

10 Quick Questions a Day | www.lizardlearning.com

1. Rewrite the sentence/s with the correct **punctuation** and **spelling**:
at long larst won morning the prize fromm the compertition that pippa had enterd and one had arrivved in her leterbox she was so exsited that she did three things cawlled her frendes took a photoe of it and hid it in her room when her pairents arrivved home they asekd pippa a cuple of things what had she one and where it was _____
_____
_____
_____
_____
_____

2. *A phrase is a group of words without a verb. Many phrases start with a preposition.* Write the **phrases** in this sentence: His nails were dirty from digging in the garden so he carefully washed his hands with soap and water. _____
_____

3. *Plurals are words that mean more than one.* Change **octopi** to **singular** form: _____

4. *Can you remember the meaning of antonyms to complete this question?*
Write the definition of **antonyms**: _____

5. Write the missing **vowels**:   m __ r m __ r   d __ c __ p t __ __ n
   s __ rf __ c __   s c __ __ n c __   j __ __ r n __ l   s __ r g __ __ n

6. What time does the teacher's clock show right now? _____
What will be the time **48 hours** from now? _____
314 days = _____ weeks _____ days

7. *Exponents (e.g. $4^2 = 4 \times 4 = 16$, $2^3 = 2 \times 2 \times 2 = 8$).*
$7^2 =$ ____ $3^2 =$ ____ $9^2 =$ ____ $3^2 - 2^3 =$ ____ $5^2 - 20 =$ ____

8. From the centre of the **compass** I travel north, I turn right 45° and walk through the centre. What direction am I walking? _____
Label all compass points.
What is the **magnitude** of the angle between N and SE? _____

9. Which is the most suitable unit of **measurement** (km^2, m^2 or **ha**) when measuring the area of a **farm**? _____

10. The secretary was having a very busy day. His phone rang 9 times within a 30 minute period. If his day continued to be this busy, how many times will his phone ring in three hours? _____

| Name: | Date: | Year: |

1. Rewrite the sentence/s with the correct **punctuation** and **spelling**:
   phillips howse was barly visible from the road becourse the trees and bushs in theyre front yard werre so tall and dense the trees prevented visiters from estableshing if a house was there what colour it was and hoo lived there the trees were home to siveral birds ravens kookabarras and roselles _____
   _____
   _____
   _____
   _____

2. **Can you remember the meaning of adjectives to complete this question?**
   Write the definition of **adjectives**: _____

3. Locate the incorrectly spelled words. Write them correctly: extrordinary / aeronautical / breezily / cautiosly _____

4. Which definition best describes **disturbance:** _____
   a) one who has a compulsive habit of disturbing things.
   b) the interruption of a settled and peaceful condition.

5. Write six words. Make one the **odd** one out. *Test someone near you:* _____
   _____

6. What time does the teacher's clock show right now? _____
   What will be the time **70 hours and 37 minutes** from now? _____
   5 centuries = _____ years   **19 weeks** = _____ days   _____ days in **Autumn**
   On day 1 of a road trip I drove **382km in 4hr** and on day 2, I drove **354km in 4hr**.
   What was my **average speed** over the two days? _____

7. Write the **value** of 3 in these numbers: 64 139 756 _____ 906 421.03 _____

8.
    ```
      9_53          8_16          66_4          6_18
    - 49_2        - 421_        + _817        - _649
    ------        ------        ------        ------
      4951          3805          9501          4369
    ```

9. Which **3D shape** could have this top view?  _____

10. The Anderson family, consisting of 3 children and 2 adults were all going to the cinema. Adult's tickets cost $19.70 and children's tickets cost $12.60. How much was it going to cost for the family to go to the movies? _____

Name: _____ Date: _____ Year: _____

1. Rewrite the sentence/s with the correct **punctuation** and **spelling**:
   the keybords keys were so fillthy that u culd hardley make owt the letterrs and cymbols printed on them is that an A or M suzy was looking hard at the keys to sea if she culd werk out the differennce its definitely an A she worked out and quetly sed to hersef _____
   _____
   _____
   _____

2. *A subordinate clause adds meaning to a principle clause. It cannot be used by itself. It needs the principal clause (e.g. I have to help my little cousin with colouring in, as she can't keep within the lines).* Use the boxes below to draw a line to the **matching clause**:

Main Clause	Subordinate Clause
My little brother loves copying me,	because the moon was only a thin crescent.
It was a pitch black night,	so I have to watch what I do.

3. **Can you remember the meaning of apostrophes of ownership to complete this question?**
   Write six examples of an **apostrophe of ownership** of groups: _____
   _____

4. *A metaphor is when we compare two things but we say one thing is the other (e.g. the sea is an angry dog).* Write a **metaphor** that you already know:
   _____

5. **Can you remember the meaning of rhetorical questions to complete this question?**
   Write which sentence is a **rhetorical question**: _____
         a) Why do I even bother?   b) Can you be bothered doing it?

6. What time does the teacher's clock show right now?_____
   What will be the time **47 minutes** from now? _____ If the day is **Thursday** and the time is **4:05pm**, what day and time is it in **120 hours**? _____

7. The computer I want to buy is available at 2 different stores. One is advertising it for $1000 less 10%, the other store has it advertised at $1200 with a 20% discount. Which is the better offer? _____

8. **< means less than > means greater than = equal to**
   47 324 ☐ 37 219   649 023 ☐ 1 207 024

9. Name this **3D object**:_____

10. Brad has a rain tank that holds 850L. He estimates that there is 675L currently in the tank. How many more litres are needed to fill the tank? _____

Name: _____ Date: _____ Year: _____

1. Rewrite the sentence/s with the correct **punctuation** and **spelling**:
   have you ever aspirred to be taller well their is actualy a way you can be but there is ownly won small problm you need two fined yorself a spacship apparentley humens grow a little tawller in space becuse there is know gravity puling down on them _____
   _____
   _____
   _____

2. *A phrase is a group of words without a verb. Many phrases start with a preposition.*
   Write the **phrases** in this sentence: _____
   He threw the ball towards me and at the same time yelled, "Catch!"

3. *Can you remember the meaning of compound words to complete this question?*
   Write a sentence that includes two **compound** words: _____
   _____

4. *Synonyms are words that have similar meanings.* Think of six words. *Test someone on their knowledge of synonyms that would match!* _____
   _____

5. *Rhetorical questions are asked when an answer is not needed (e.g. Why would anyone hurt an animal?).* Write your own **rhetorical question**: _____
   _____

6. What time does the teacher's clock show right now? _____
   What will be the time **440 minutes** from now? _____
   16.1 years = _____ weeks   How many **seconds** in one hour? _____
   There are **1440 minutes** in a day. How many **minutes** in one week? _____
   Speed = distance ÷ time. How far did I travel if I drove **9.25km/hr** for **7 days**? _____

7. Find **50%** of: $21 _____   56 _____ $70 _____ $32.50 _____

8. _890_   27
   + 5_0_3   5)123.5   8)3648   × 15
   _____   _____
   100994

9. Write 2 things you could **measure** in **micrograms**: _____
   _____

10. Each member of the McKenzie family had a carry-on bag – the airline allowed everyone 20kg each: Dad had 18kg, mum 19.25kg, John 17kg and Peggy 19.95kg. What was their combined allowance? _____ How many kgs did they have spare? _____

Answers

Year 1 - *Page 8*
1. My grandma lives in Melbourne.
2. describing
3. heads
4. The buzzing bee stung my friend.
5. A
6. adult to direct, adult to check
7. 2, 11, 12, 13, 22
8. 2+**10**=12
9. A
10. 13 kittens left in the box.

Year 1 - *Page 9*
1. He was a farmer who grew lettuce, carrots and peas.
2. which
3. adult to check
4. dinner
5. various answers, adult to check
6. adult to direct, adult to check
7. 12 even, 7 odd
8. triangle 20
9. various answers, adult to check
10. 20 dragons

Year 1 - *Page 10*
1. The vase was old and had a crack, a chip, a scratch and a mark on it.
2. various answers, adult to check
3. did
4. night
5. animal, an, and, a
6. adult to direct, adult to check
7. 7 more candles
8. 29, **30**, **31**, 32
9. 30
10. 25 apples

Year 1 - *Page 11*
1. The lamp was pretty with a huge yellow shade.
2. monster
3. couldn't
4. brake
5. various answers, adult to check *e.g. monkey, mouse*
6. adult to direct, adult to check
7. 9+10=19 fish
8. Billy
9. various answers, adult to check, various answers, adult to check
10. 19 cups

Year 1 - *Page 12*
1. Can you quickly come here Penny?
2. cut
3. sea/flea
4. **a** trolley, **a** ride, **an** ape, **the** ride, **the** trolley, **the** ape
5. various answers, adult to check *e.g. bananas, bread*
6. adult to direct, adult to check
7. 5
8. various answers, adult to check
9.
10. 13 oranges

Year 1 - *Page 13*
1. He opened the front door and the dog jumped up on him.
2. various answers, adult to check e.g. big
3. skip**ping**
4. A
5. various answers, adult to check *e.g. **o**rangutan, **o**strich*
6. adult to direct, adult to check
7. 8, $8
8. **9 + 6** = 15
9. August
10. 17 ties

Year 1 - *Page 14*
1. The babies of a kangaroo and a koala are called joeys.
2. bedroom
3. various answers, adult to check *e.g. it's (it is)*
4. noisy
5. various answers *e.g. were, weren't, dare, aren't, dad, don't, isn't*
6. adult to direct, adult to check
7. 7 + 8 = 15, 4 + 9 = 13, 6 + 6 = 12
8. 2, A
9. various answers for both, adult to check
10. 72 boats

Year 1 - *Page 15*
1. Paula couldn't stop laughing because it was such a funny movie.
2. various answers, adult to check *e.g. red*
3. bowl**s**, run**s**, tree**s**
4. speak
5. **thr**ee
6. adult to direct, adult to check
7. 5 cents
8. **14 + 4** = 18
9. various answers, adult to check
10. 81 cherries

Year 1 - *Page 16*
1. Watch out for the cars!
2. cough
3. house**s**
4. narrow
5. various answers, adult to check
6. adult to direct, adult to check
7. 9, 20, 30
8. 35, thirty-five
9. A
10. 59 crabs

Year 1 - *Page 17*
1. Their house had three bedrooms.
2. pull
3. batter, chatter, patter, scatter
4. A
5. V, E, F, G, J
6. adult to direct, adult to check
7. 37, 22 + 15 = 37
8. various answers, adult to check picture
9. various answers for both, adult to check
10. 29 flowers

Year 2 - *Page 20*
1. Chickens are birds, but don't fly much, and emus can't fly at all.
2. quickly
3. drop**ping**
4. hare
5. train/1, baby/2, bulldozer/3 - baby, bulldozer, train
6. adult to direct, adult to check
7. 38 **+** 14 **=** 52, 52 birds
8. 697 + 102 = **799**
9. adult to check
10. 7 milk bottles

Year 2 - *Page 21*
1. Hey you!
2. down
3. uncover
4. Mason used the white paper to write a note.
5. various answers, adult to check *e.g. bait, rod, sunscreen*
6. adult to direct, 6 hours and 15 minutes or 6 and one quarter hours
7. 13, 69, 97
8. 13 birthdays, various answers
9.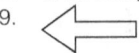
10. $2, $1.50

Year 2 - *Page 22*
1. "In June, I'm going to get a new bike," replied Charlie.
2. various answers, adult to check *e.g. lion, clown, juggler*
3. have
4. a/the plane, an elephant, a/the shop
5. K
6. adult to direct, adult to check
7. 2 groups of 4 papers = **8**, **2 x 4 = 8**, adult to check
8. various answers, adult to check *e.g. 5, 10, 15, 20 - counting forwards in 5's*
9. various answers, adult to check *e.g. window, whiteboard*
10. 6 groups

Year 2 - *Page 23*
1. The children saw the bear scratching his back on the tree by the river.
2. various answers, adult to check *e.g. jumping, sleeping, snoring*
3. future
4. A
5. various answers *e.g. weren't, were, to, maze, present, sent*
6. adult to direct, 60 min
7. 13, 10, 3, 13
8. triangle
9. oval ◯, circle ◯, hexagon ⬡
10. 31 days

Year 2 - *Page 24*
1. Birds can be many colours, such as green, blue, red and even rainbow coloured.
2. various answers, adult to check *e.g. blue, stormy*
3. lighthouse
4. various answers, adult to discuss
5. **We**d**n**e**s**day
6. adult to direct, adult to check
7. fifth
8. various answers, adult to check *e.g. impossible, unlikely*
9. 0 corners, various answers e.g
10. 40 children

Year 2 - *Page 25*
1. "The dog just bit me!" yelled Joseph.
2. squeak
3. isn't
4. various answers, adult to check *e.g. happy/joyful*
5. various answers, adult to check

Answers

6. adult to direct, adult to check
7. 84, 94
8. various answers, adult to check
   e.g. 13 = 6 + 7, 19 = 10 + 9
9. November
10. 59 lollies

Year 2 - Page 26
1. "I'm not well," Harry said to his teacher Mrs Roberts.
2. various answers, adult to check
   e.g. his, her
3. heard
4. various answers, adult to check
   e.g. cold/hot
5. ice cream
6. adult to direct, adult to check
7. 976 + 8 = **984**, 35 - 10 = **25**,
   419 + 43 = **462**, 476 - 8 = **468**
8. salad wrap, 7
9. flipped
10. 6 groups

Year 2 - Page 27
1. The beach was very very dark at night, but they weren't scared.
2. various answers, adult to check
   e.g. quickly, sadly, happily
3. dress**ed** / various answers, adult to check
   e.g. The mother dressed her little boy in a jumper.
4. heel
5. quick
6. adult to direct, 12 hours
7. 17 + 7 = **24**, 34 - 17 = **17**,
   34 - 7 = **27**, 7 + 17 = **24**
8. **798**, 799, **800**
9. soccer field
10. 21 boys

Year 2 - Page 28
1. Kangaroos, wallabies, koalas and wombats are not domestic animals that live in our backyards as pets.
2. over
3. **im**possible
4. I like to drink water when it is hot.
5. various answers, adult to check
   e.g. cricket bat, ball, pads
6. adult to direct, 16 hours
7. 4th
8. 483
9. adult to check
10. 32 uniforms

Year 2 - Page 29
1. Stop shouting!
2. various answers, adult to check drawing
   e.g. monkeys, tigers
3. those
4. a, an
5. H, L, R, V
6. adult to direct, adult to check
7.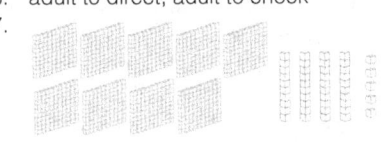
8. various answers, adult to check drawing
9. circles, rectangles, squares, triangle
10. 20 grapes

Year 3 - Page 32
1. Once upon a time a fairy lived in a magic land far, far away.
2. Proper nouns are the actual names of people, places, animals or things.
3. crack**ing**, crack**er**, crack**ed**
4. various answers e.g.
   dribble: to dribble food from your mouth
   dribble: to move a ball on a stick, you can dribble a ball in hockey
5. each
6. adult to direct, adult to check
7.
8. 7, No (Colin - 10, Sandra - 14)
9. 5
10. 34

Year 3 - Page 33
1. The smallest bone in the human body can be found in the ear.
2. places, animals or things
3. various answers - adult to check
   e.g. bluebottle, sandcastle
4. bored, ball
5. teacher
6. adult to direct, 10:55am

7. 6211
8. 750, 650, 550
9. D
10. 3 groups

Year 3 - Page 34
1. Pearl waved goodbye to her parents.
2. A pronoun is a word that takes the place of a noun (e.g. her, him, its, themselves).
3. women, teachers, uncles
4. your
5. adult to check
6. adult to direct, adult to check
7. 42, 888, 316, 502, 4722
8. one - once, two - three times, three - twice, four - twice, five - twice, six - three times
9. 100cm
10. no, 31

Year 3 - Page 35
1. Marilyn had three little brothers called Mike, Ben and Billy.
2. she
3. let us
4. lost
5. dangerous, curious, fluffier
6. adult to direct,

7. 714
8.
9.
10. 29°C

Year 3 - Page 36
1. Phillipa loved the stories that her grandmother would tell her at bedtime each night.
2. stories, tries, ladies
3. A pronoun is a word that takes the place of a noun (e.g. her, him, its, themselves).
4. too
5. adventure, ordinary, table, travel
6. adult to direct, adult to check
7. true
8. 600, 700, 800, 900, 1000
9. stick B
10. 143

Year 3 - Page 37
1. Mum gave me a gingerbread man, a glass of milk and a banana for afternoon tea.
2. An adverb is a word which modifies or adds meaning to a verb, adjective or adverb by telling how, when, why or where a thing is done.
3. **un**tangle, **pre**paid, **un**paid, **in**side
4. raise: rays, raze / hire: higher
   various answers e.g.
   rays: The rays of the sun.
   raise: I hope to raise all three puppies.
   raze: They had to raze the building.
   hire: I want to hire a butler.
   higher: He went higher than me on the swing.
5. boat
6. adult to direct, adult to check
7. 600 - 95 = **505**, 300 - 42 = **258**,
   1376 + 948 = **2324**, 8604 + 1798 = **10402**
8. various answers, adult to check
9. jug
10. 5 goldfish

Year 3 - Page 38
1. Kate went to the lake and saw three frogs, two lizards, five birds and six fish.
2. you
3. wriggle, delightful
4. ugly
5. various answers, adult to check
6. adult to direct,

7.
8. strawberry, A
9. 30 days have September April, June and November. All the rest have 31 except for February alone, which has 28 days clear but 29 days in each leap year.
10. 17 kilograms

Year 3 - Page 39
1. "Don't forget your hat, ball and spade!" called Sandra's dad.
2. was sweeping
3. sail**boat**, in**to**, see**saw**
4. two,
   various answers, adult to check
5. dried, dry, dry
6. adult to direct, adult to check
7. 5007
8. least: 2 and 3, most: 5
9. Sunday, 4, Sunday
10. 16 boys

Year 3 - Page 40
1. "Ava, would you bring that to me please?" asked Mrs Aldred.
2. correctly
3. various answers, adult to check
   e.g. he hasn't had breakfast and his mother isn't happy

Answers

4. false/untrue
5. fifty, fight, o'clock, plant
6. adult to direct, hours
7. [bar diagram]
8. $4 \times \mathbf{5} = 20$, $48 \div 6 = \mathbf{8}$, $\mathbf{28} \div 7 = 4$, $81 \div \mathbf{9} = 9$, $\mathbf{3} \times 8 = 24$, $\mathbf{3} \div 3 = 1$, $6 \times \mathbf{7} = 42$, $14 \div \mathbf{2} = 7$, $56 \div \mathbf{7} = 8$
9. [rectangular prism]
10. 9 eggs

Year 3 - Page 41
1. 'Did you know dinosaurs had many bones in their bodies," added the museum scientist.
2. she, I
3. various answers, adult to check
   e.g. pencils, books, rulers
4. lucky
5. clothes, coat, delighted, hammer
6. adult to direct, 02:20
7. $10 \times 4 = \mathbf{40}$, $7 \times 2 = \mathbf{14}$, $8 \times 5 = \mathbf{40}$, $3 \times 8 = \mathbf{24}$
8. No. There is only one plane and one hotrod so it would be least likely to land on either of those.
9. B
10. 25 stickers

Year 4 - Page 44
1. "Get out of my room Jake!" Kym screamed to her brother every time he tried entering her room.
2. inside
3. various answers, adult to check
   e.g apple: apples, lady: ladies
4. Antonyms are words that are opposites.
5. [word search grid] pedal, petrol, gearstick, birthday
6. adult to direct, adult to check, 8:50, **9:20**, 9:50, 10:20
7. 3 214
8. tractor
9. varies every leap year, 1st April
10. various answers e.g. 699 apples on the tree and 123 in the bucket. How many altogether? 822 apples

Year 4 - Page 45
1. Marie's father was a fireman at the local fire station.
2. various answers
   e.g. We went fishing at the pond.
3. various answers
   e.g. board**games**, some**thing**, friend**ship**
4. various answers, adult to check
   e.g. walk/ramble/stroll
5. b, c, d, f, g, h, j, k, l, m, n, p, q, r, s, t, v, w, x, y, z
6. adult to direct, adult to check, 132 months, 11 years
7. various answers
   e.g. 396 - 96 = 300, 96 + 300 = 396
8. NSW
9. Monday, twice
10. $66

Year 4 - Page 46
1. The cows, horses and chickens were locked away in their paddock and chicken coop at night.
2. no, their
3. woman - **women**, teacher - **teachers**, uncle - **uncles**
4. the, the, a, an
5. various answers, adult to check
   e.g. sell / I will sell
6. adult to direct, adult to check, 9 months
7. $\frac{1}{10}$
8. $\frac{40}{100}$ $\frac{41}{100}$ $\frac{42}{100}$ $\frac{\mathbf{43}}{\mathbf{100}}$ $\frac{\mathbf{44}}{\mathbf{100}}$ $\frac{45}{100}$ $\frac{\mathbf{46}}{\mathbf{100}}$
9. 6, 9
10.

30	16	26
20	24	28
22	32	18

Year 4 - Page 47
1. When you arrive at a hotel, the concierge takes your bags from your car to your room.
2. farmer, rounded, milking
3. let us, we shall (will)
4. A
5. I was in my bedroom reading a book when dad came in and said goodnight to me.
6. adult to direct, adult to check, 10:55, **11:00**, 11:05, 11:10, **11:15**, 11:20
7. $6
8. 8, 2, 12
9. $4 \times 3 = 12cm^2$
10. 4 giraffes

Year 4 - Page 48
1. They really didn't know what to do. The storm was raging, but all the animals were still outside and were becoming more distressed.
2. A pronoun is a word that takes the place of a noun (e.g. her, him, it, themselves).
3. glkisnpar - **sparkling**, adjective
4. **allowed:** The child was allowed to go to the movies.
   aloud: John sang out aloud.
5. various answers, adult to check
6. adult to direct, adult to check, 48 months, 4 years 0 months
7. 4, 12 - 4 = 8 then 8 ÷ 2 = 4
8. 2
9. 250**mL**, 320**mL**, 750**mL**, 20**L**
10. 109 metres

Year 4 - Page 49
1. The soccer team would practise every Monday afternoon for their Saturday game.
2. A prolonged period of abnormally low rainfall, leading to a shortage of water.
3. crumb, number, member
4. various answer adult to check
   e.g. chair/seat, bang/noise
5. various answers e.g. proud, curry, ringlet, second, buoy, do, skin, king, building, ladder
6. adult to direct, adult to check, 15:15, 15:10, 15:05, 15:00, **14:55**
7. 6178 - 183 = 5 995
8. New South Wales, Victoria, Tasmania, South Australia, Australian Capital Territory
9. A jam jar: **mL**, A bathtub: **L**

10. various answers, adult to check
    e.g. There were 613 nuts on the tree and 599 were harvested. How many nuts are left on the tree? 14 nuts

Year 4 - Page 50
1. Giants are just not found in fairytale stories and myths. In fact in Turkey, there is a man who is more than 2 and a half metres tall.
2. A preposition is a word used before a noun or a pronoun to show its relationship to some other word in the sentence; it is used to make a phrase (e.g. under the box, in the box, on the box, by, up, down, near, through, over, at).
3. various answers, adult to check
4. various answers
   Wear: Joshua has to wear red for his sport's carnival.
   Where: Where did I leave my keys?
5. various answers, adult to check
   e.g. co**nt**ain, re**t**ain, se**ve**re, **up**stairs
6. adult to direct, adult to check, 15:10, **15:20**, 15:30, **15:40**, 15:50
7. True, False
8. $3\overline{)27} = 9$, $8\overline{)72} = 9$, $8\overline{)32} = 4$, $11\overline{)99} = 9$, $7\overline{)77} = 11$, $9\overline{)108} = 12$, $9\overline{)63} = 7$
9. 9L, 7L, 4.5L, 1.264L
10. 289 eggs

Year 4 - Page 51
1. I asked my grandmother when she was born. She said, "1943."
2. octopus - **common noun**, elephant - **common noun**, Monday - **proper noun**, roses - **common noun**
3. various answers, adult to check
4. There are three articles: the, a and an. The, is a definite article (e.g. give me the cup). A, is an indefinite article (e.g. give me a cup. This would be any cup). An, is the article to use before a vowel (e.g. an umbrella).
5. fifth, oblong, October, plumber, quadrilateral, quotient
6. adult to direct, adult to check, 134 months, 11 years 2 months
7. a) $\frac{2}{7}$, b) $\frac{7}{12}$
8. B
9. 6kg, 4 213g
10. $36 \div 9 = 4$

Year 4 - Page 52
1. "Bamboo is one of the fastest growing plants," the gardener was telling her customer.
2. various answers e.g. I waited patiently for the clown to make my balloon.
3. rethink
4. the, a
5. various answers
6. adult to direct, adult to check, 71 months
7. 2 cups of orange juice, $\frac{3}{4}$ cup frozen raspberries, $\frac{3}{4}$ cup frozen blueberries, 18 strawberries halved
8. [sports balls: soccer, football, basketball, basketball, soccer, football]
9. $7\frac{1}{2}$L = **7 500mL**, $4\frac{1}{2}$L = **4 500mL**, $5\frac{1}{2}$L = **5 500mL**, 1 362L = **1 362 000mL**
10. $24 \div 4 =$ **6 notes**

Answers

Year 4 - *Page 53*
1. "Look at that rainbow! It has beautiful colours!" noticed Danielle.
2. shattering, *adult to discuss*
3. ficultifd - **difficult**, gealliv - **village**, qiliud - **liquid**, preimu - **umpire**
4. homophone
5. various answers, adult to check
6. adult to direct, adult to check, **17:44**, 17:41, 17:38, 17:35, 17:32
7. *First Way:* 0x5=0, 1x5=5, 2x5=10, 3x5=15, 4x5=20, 5x5=25, 6x5=30, 7x5=35, 8x5=40, 8x5=45, 10x5=50, 11x5=55, 12x5=60
Turnaround Way: 0÷5=0, 5÷5=1, 10÷5=2, 15÷5=3, 20÷5=4, 25÷5=5, 30÷5=6, 35÷5=7, 40÷5=8, 45÷5=9, 50÷5=10, 55÷5=11, 6-÷5=12
8. 3)**36** = 12, 6)**54** = 9, 7)**56** = 8, 7)**63** = 9, **8**)88 = 11, 9)108 = **12**, 5)**45** = 9
9. 8 000g, 4 500g
10. 1 385 - 873 = 512

Year 5 - *Page 56*
1. Ms Potts's lunches were always yummy.
2. various answers, adult to check *e.g. John, with an arm load of heavy groceries, stumbled up the stairs*
3. various answers, adult to check *e.g. blackboard, whiteboard*
4. raise
5. a e i o u
6. adult to direct, adult to check, 1yr 7mths
7. *First Way:* 0x8=0, 1x8=8, 2x8=16, 3x8=24, 4x8=32, 5x8=40, 6x8=48, 7x8=56, 8x8=64, 9x8=72, 10x8=80, 11x8=88, 12x8=96
Turnaround Way: 0÷8=0, 8÷8=1, 16÷8=2, 24÷8=3, 32÷8=4, 40÷8=5, 48÷8=6, 56÷8=7, 64÷8=8, 72÷8=9, 80÷8=10, 88÷8=11, 96÷8=12
8. three hundred and forty-three **less than** (<) 354, 9.54 **greater than** (>) $9\frac{1}{2}$, $7.50 **less than** (<) seven and three quaters
9.
10. 12 packs

Year 5 - *Page 57*
1. Ian could never remember if the postcode for his house was 3 058 or 3 057. "Which one is it?" he asked his mum.
2. great surprise
3. it's = correct, you're = incorrect should be your
4. various answers, adult to check *e.g. flour/flower*
5. various answers, adult to check
6. adult to direct, adult to check
7. 900, 300, 400, 1 000, 3 200
8. various answers, adult to check
9. 27cm²
10. $16.60

Year 5 - *Page 58*
1. I've never understood how, if the Earth's round and always turning, we don't fall off. I realise it's because of gravity but I'm still not sure how it works.
2. fish paste - **common**, water - **common**, Sydney - **proper**, Japan - **proper**, house - **common**, Max - **proper**, Little Miss Muffet - **proper**, St James - **proper**
3. weak, holiday, family
4. Antonyms are words that are opposites.
5. The children in the park were playing when one of them fell and broke his arm.
6. adult to direct, adult to check, 02:05
7. 3 392 039
8. various answers, adult to check
9. True, False 9cm²
10. no, $5.50

Year 5 - *Page 59*
1. "Apples 99 cents!" A kilo of oranges $3.99!" they could hear the fruiterer calling out his bargain specials, from the top end of the shopping centre.
2. will be swimming
3. kilograms, noun
4. Synonyms are words that have similar meanings.
5. various answers, adult to check
6. adult to direct, adult to check
7. 5 428 - 5 000 = 428
8. Perth:1,D / Hobart: 5,F / 3 states
9. 155°
10. 220mm

Year 5 - *Page 60*
1. The netball coach wasn't happy with Cindy when she missed the net again because she knew Cindy wasn't trying, "Come on!" she called from across the court.
2. onto, for, in
3. one, able, travel, across, universe
4. an, the, the
5. various answers, adult to check
6. adult to direct, adult to check, 118 weeks 5 days
7. 2.43
8. $\frac{9}{4}, \frac{21}{5}, \frac{11}{4}, \frac{15}{2}, \frac{12}{5}$
9. m²
10. 152.2cm, 1.522m

Year 5 - *Page 61*
1. The gold fish in the pond liked to blow bubbles. When you walk past them they look up at you from the water. I think they are waiting for food.
2. wanted, broke, to go shopping (infinitive verb)
3. various answers, adult to check *e.g. chain**saw**, rain**fall**, **toad**stool*
4. A
5. flowers, sinister, evil, monster
6. adult to direct, adult to check
7. 1 483 848
8. 4.5kg, 13kg
9. pentagon or prism
10. 4m x 3m or 2m x 6m, 1m x 12m is not possible

Year 5 - *Page 62*
1. Each morning at shift changeover, the nurses' station was full of specialists, physiotherapists, nutritionists and of course nurses. It was important that each person was there at 7am to discuss the patients' progress from the night before.
2. walk - **common noun**, dog - **common noun**, Steep Hill Road - **proper noun**, James - **proper noun**, street - **common noun**, Brisbane - **proper noun**
3. loud
4. Antonyms are words that are opposites.
5. various answers, adult to check
6. adult to direct, adult to check
7. 0.7, 0.6, 0.5, **0.4**, **0.3**, **0.2**, **0.1**, 0
8. one thousand and eighty-nine **less than** (<) 1 890,
0.64 **greater than** (>) $\frac{46}{100}$,
4.73 **less than** (<) $4\frac{3}{4}$,
$17.48 **less than** (<) seventeen and a half,
48 392 **greater than** (>) forty-eight thousand, three hundred and twenty-nine
9. 1 214cm, 3 600mm
10. 2.1m

Year 5 - *Page 63*
1. It had been raining for days, and Paula wondered when it would stop. She wanted to ride her bike from Aspley to Caboolture, but wasn't about to do that whole circuit in a downpour of rain.
2. various answers, adult to check *e.g. style, cut, trim, perm*
3. toe**s**, planet**s**, photo**s**, change**s**, canvas**es**
4. various answers, adult to check *e.g. friend - **enemy**, easy - **hard**, careful - **careless**, warm - **cool**, allowed - **prohibited/stopped**, disagree - **agree**, healthy - **unhealthy/ill/sick***
5. ache, oblique, overboard, perimeter, swam
6. adult to direct, adult to check, 6:05pm
7. $38.53 + $26.79 = **$65.32**; $41.25 - $37.77 = **$ 3.48**; $17.03 x 4 = **$69.12**; $12.46 x 8 = **$99.68**
8. Papua New Guinea or Indonesia, Arafura Sea
9. 2 x (L + W) = 2 x (15cm) = **30cm**
10. 35cm

Year 5 - *Page 64*
1. "That's gross!" yelled Sonia at Dominika. Dominika had tricked her. Sonya hadn't realised the lolly that she had given her was very very sour instead of sweet.
2. exhausted
3. various answers, adult to check *e.g. bathtub, lightbulb*
4. Synonyms are words that have similar meanings.
5. various answers, e.g. information, formation, index, symmetry, yard/s, astonish, equipment, tight
6. adult to direct, adult to check, 28 minutes
7. 9 units or ones
8. various answers, adult to check
9. 6.019kg
10. 21°C

Year 5 - *Page 65*
1. On the television monitors at the space station, a red spot became visible on the satellite system. It appeared to the astronauts that their maybe an alien spacecraft nearby. On closer look, it was just a speck of dust.
2. A pronoun is a word that takes the place of a noun (e.g. her, him, it, themselves).

Answers

3. adjust, fright, friends, station
4. calmness, endurance
5. various answers e.g. location, frustration, dictionary, endurance, satellite
6. adult to direct, adult to check, 50 years
7. 28 bull dogs
8. 38 492 **equal to (=)** 38 000 + 492,
   one thousand, four hundred and sixty **not equal (≠)** 146,
   285 **equal to (=)** two hundred and eighty-five,
   $1.50 **not equal (≠)** $0.50 $0.50 $0.10 $0.10 $0.05
9. cylinder
10. 540g

Year 6 - Page 68
1. Her baby was 3 years old and she so badly wanted her daughter to be baptised at the local church. The mother finally found a wonderful church called St. John's Church. The priest's name was Father Thomas Shepard, who welcomed the two lovingly into his church.
2. various answers e.g. in the dazzling light, the bubbling stream rippled over the stones
3. various answers, adult to check e.g. eggshell, hairbrush
4. various answers e.g. words that are similar joy/happy
5.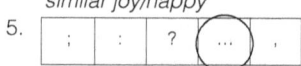
6. adult to direct, adult to check, 5 decades
7. division must be done first a) 40 b) 22
8.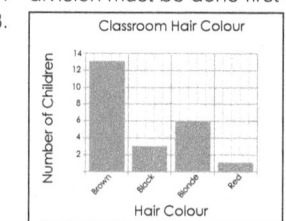
9. 3:15pm
10. 33 per day; 5 (school week) x 33 = **165 sandwiches**

Year 6 - Page 69
1. "Get out!" Mavis screamed at the dirty dog who was walking mud through the house.
2. various answers, adult to check e.g. involving many carefully arranged parts or details, detailed and complicated in design and planning
3. Contractions are shortened forms of two words
4. an, the
5. 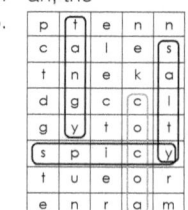 spicy, salty, tangy, cocoa
6. adult to direct, adult to check, 56 years old
7. 1, 2, 3, 4, 6, 8, 12, 16, 24, 48
8. 1, 8, 27, 64, **125**, **216**, **343**, **512**, **729**
   Rule: the cube of counting numbers from 1-9
9. 68 cm²
10. $18 was the individual contribution

Year 6 - Page 70
1. The two horses were locked away in the stables until the storm cleared. The stables' assistant was constantly talking to the horses calmly saying, "There, there, it's alright boys. The thunder and lightening will stop soon and then you can gallop around the meadows again."
2. yet
3. equivalent, linguist
4. various answers, adult to check e.g. The ocean was <u>as</u> still <u>as</u> the calm before the storm.
5. various answers, adult to check e.g e**ducation**, **au**thorise, re**gulation**, pre**caution**
6. adult to direct, adult to check, 11 hours 9 minutes
7. 4 x 10 000 000 = **40 000 000**
8. Blue - 𝍫𝍫 III   White - 𝍫𝍫 𝍫𝍫 IIII
   Red - 𝍫𝍫 𝍫𝍫 𝍫𝍫 𝍫𝍫 III   Silver - 𝍫𝍫 𝍫𝍫 𝍫𝍫 II
   Green - 𝍫𝍫 IIII   Yellow - IIII   Black - 𝍫𝍫 𝍫𝍫 I
9. cm³
10. $30

Year 6 - Page 71
1. The children demonstrated incredible initiative in writing a play entitled, 'Adopt a Pet.'
2. various answers, adult to check e.g. Bruteous was Jono's rad mutt that jumped into the back of his ute in one large leap.
3. various answers adult to check
4. ahead
5. hated, hate, will hate / negotiated, negotiate, will negotiate / mourned, mourn, will mourn / fixed, fix, will fix / typed, type, will type / yelled, yell, will/ shall yell
6. adult to direct, adult to check, 9 weeks 0 days
7. 738 - 538 = 200, 738 ÷ 3 - 46 = 200, (738 - 338) ÷ 2 = 200
8. $\frac{3}{8}$ **equal to (=)** 0.375, $\frac{3}{4}$ **equal to (=)** 0.75, $\frac{1}{2}$ **not equal to (≠)** 0.25
9. 378 m³
10. 8 years

Year 6 - Page 72
1. The photographer's job at a wedding can be very stressful. The event happens only once, and the photographer needs to be able to capture all the bride's and groom's most significant moments in a skillful and artistic way.
2. Various answers, adult to check e.g. The cat crept cautiously and silently across the lawn.
3. various answers, adult to check e.g. classroom, doorway, woodwork
4. various answers e.g. enchanted - **enthralled**, swathe - **wrap**, traverse - **cross**, compound - **intensify,** foundation - **basis,** endurance - **toleration**
5. A
6. adult to direct, adult to check, $\frac{1}{25}$
7. $27.85
8. 18 ÷ (**3 x 1**) = 6, 24 ÷ (**8 ÷ 2**) = 6
   20 = 12 + (**16 ÷ 2**)
9.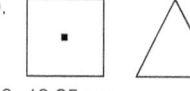
10. 13.35 cm

Year 6 - Page 73
1. Lila was watching a documentary on cheetahs. She'd never seen an animal move so fast. It was incredible! She told her mum that cheetas were, in fact, the fastest animals on Earth, also the best looking. "What's that saying, faster than the speed of light?" she commented.
2. various answers, adult to check e.g. beautiful, angry
3. catiotmua - **automatic**, suapllebi - **plausible**, fulnmour - **mournful**, notirpeucua - **precaution**
4. malfunction
5. It is sometimes difficult to remember the steps involved in opening up a new document on the computer.
6. adult to direct, adult to check, 04:45
7.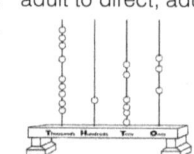
8. 12, 15, 18, 21, **24**, **27**, **30**, **33**, **36**
   Rule: counting in 3's or adding 3 each time
9. metres
10. $\frac{3}{15}$
    Fraction: $\frac{1}{5}$, Decimal: 0.2, Percentage: 20%

Year 6 - Page 74
1. At long last one morning the prize from the competition that Pippa had entered and won, had arrived in her letterbox. She was so excited that she did three things: called her friends, took a photo of it and hid it in her room. When her parents arrived home, they asked Pippa a couple of things … what had she won and where it was.
2. in the garden, with soap and water
3. octopus
4. Antonyms are words that are opposites.
5. m**ur**mur, de**cep**tion, s**ur**face, s**ci**ence, j**our**nal, s**ur**geon
6. adult to direct, adult to check, 44 weeks 6 days
7. 7² = **49**, 3² = **9**, 9² = **81**, 3² - 2³ = **1**, 5² - 20 = **5**
8. SW,
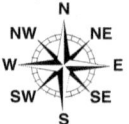
135°
9. ha
10. 54 times

Year 6 - Page 75
1. Phillip's house was barely visible from the road, because the trees and bushes in their front yard were so tall and dense. The trees prevented visitors from establishing: if a house was there, what colour it was and who lived there. The trees were home to several birds: ravens, kookaburras and rosellas.
2. Adjectives are describing words.
3. extraordinary, cautiously
4. B
5. various answers
6. adult to direct, adult to check, 500 years, 133 days, 92 days in Autumn, 92km/hr

Answers

7. 3 tens of thousands or 30 thousand
   3 hundredths
8. 9 **8**53 - 4 9**0**2 = 4 951
   8 **0**16 - 4 211 = 3 805
   6 6**8**4 + **2** 817 = 9 501
   6 **0**18 - **1** 649 = 4 369
9. cylinder or cone
10. $77.20

Year 6 - *Page 76*

1. The keyboard's keys were so filthy that you could hardly make out the letters and symbols printed on them. "Is that an A or M?" Suzy was looking hard at the keys to see if she could work out the difference. "It's definitely an A," she worked out and quietly said to herself.
2. My little brother loves copying me, **so I have to watch what I do.**
   It was a pitch black night, **because the moon was only a thin crescent.**
3. various answers, adult to check
   e.g. doctors' conference, teachers' classrooms, the boys' locker room
4. various answers, adult to check
   e.g. all the world's a stage
5. A
6. adult to direct, adult to check,
   Tuesday, 4:05pm
7. a) Working Out: $1 000 - (10% of $1 000)
      = $900
   b) Working Out: $1 200 - (20% of $1 200)
      = $960
   = **The first offer is better**
8. 47 324 **greater than (>)** 37 219
   649 023 **less than (<)** 1 207 024
9. octagonal prism
10. 175L

Year 6 - *Page 77*

1. Have you ever aspired to be taller? Well, there is actually a way you can be…but there is only one small problem. You need to find yourself a spaceship! Apparently, humans grow a little taller in space because there is no gravity pulling down on them.
2. towards me, at the same time
3. various answers, adult to check
   e.g. The seastar and jellyfish were at the rockpool exhibit.
4. various answers
5. various answers, adult to check
   e.g. How about that for a catch?
6. adult to direct, adult to check,
   837.2 weeks, 3 600 seconds,
   10 080 minutes, 64.75km
7. $21 - **$10.50**, 56 - **28**, $70 - **$35**, $32.50 - **$16.25**
8.
   ```
     48901        24.7      456        27
   + 52093     5)123.5    8)3648    x  15
   -------                           ----
    100994                            135
                                    + 270
                                    -----
                                      405
   ```
9. various answers, adult to check *e.g. medications, dust, bacteria, feathers*
10. 80kg, 5.8kg

More Fun Resources

10 QUICK QUESTIONS A DAY

Our very popular flagship series providing 5 literacy and 5 numeracy questions every single day of the school year.

BOOTCAMP

A series of resources designed to focus on essential Punctuation and Spelling skills.

COLOURING & PUZZLE BOOK

Join the Lizard Learning CLUB

Receive free activities and teaching resources delivered direct to your inbox plus be the first to find out about new time saving tools for teachers and exclusive offers.

www.lizardlearning.com

10 Quick Questions a Day | www.lizardlearning.com

©2017 Lizard Learning Pty Ltd   ISBN: 978-1-925509-61-8

www.ingramcontent.com/pod-product-compliance
Lightning Source LLC
Chambersburg PA
CBHW050715090526

44587CB00019B/3389